Rev. Dr. Ebenezer Kyere Nkansah

IGNITE YOUR PRAYER FIRE

The Secrets of Getting God to Answer Prayers.

Author's Contact:
Email: Kyerenkansah@yahoo.com, Kyerenkansah2@gmail.com
Hopeofgloryi@yahoo.org
Website: www.hognetwork.org
Tel: +1-347-559-9329

Edited by Prince George Sagoe

Printed by West Africa Times, Inc.
9409 Ulysses Court, Burke, Va. 22015
Tel.: 571.758.0789
Email: sonnyahp@gmail.com

TABLE OF CONTENTS

91 CHAPTER SEVEN

99 CHAPTER EIGHT

107 REFERENCE

FOREWORD

I n "Ignite Your Prayer Fire, the Secrets of Getting God to Answer Prayers", Rev. Kyere Nkansah, a multifaceted preacher and teacher of God's word, presents a needed Biblical and Spiritual narrative. This book on prayer, written by Dr. Ebenezer Kyere Nkansah, is an important subject matter. All believers should discuss this topic in the light of current social challenges and follow the teachings for success. The book is written in simple language, and in a layman's format to help resolve questions concerning prayer and its efficacy for Christians. The book projects the truth of Revelation and sets out the various ways Christians must approach difficulties in life. If religious teachers refrain from preaching due to ignorance, it will have dire consequences. As referenced in the book, 1 Thessalonians 5:16-18 pray without ceasing -- Matthew 26:41. "Watch and pray so that you will not fall into temptation. The spirit is willing, but the flesh is weak.".

Dr. Nkansah is a God-fearing well-known Ghanaian minister in the Diaspora who uses many practical and current means of communication to spread the Word of God to all people. He is the founder of the Hope of Glory Network Ministries, a growing ministry in Hyattsville, Maryland. My husband and I often visit to hear the great Bible teachings shared with members, despite the distance of the commute.

Dr. Nkansah is also the founder and host of the "Hope of Glory Network" radio network, which broadcasts via many channels, including Modern Ghana, Ghana Web Radio, and a Mobile App I presently have on my smartphone. The varied programs on the station make it relevant and attractive to people of all backgrounds and walks of life. As a final point, Dr. Nkansah is a pioneer in the Telephone-Conference Ministries, which meet daily over the telephone to spread the Word of God and hold prayer meetings with people worldwide who are otherwise unable to attend a regular preaching service due to personal issues or work schedules. It was through the telephone conference ministry that I met Dr. Nkansah in 2012 when I joined his Hope of Glory Telephone Ministry. Through these avenues of worship, my family and I can fellowship with God twice daily: in the early morning at 5:00 AM, at 9:00 PM, and throughout the day via radio broadcast. That has dramatically helped with my spiritual growth in Christ.

Dr. Nkansah's ministry continues to grow every day. It is attracting a younger audience than his counterparts because of the channels and ways he proclaims the Word of God, prays and teaches the Bible to his audience. Dr. Nkansah's way of sharing the Gospel is akin to Paul's work for the church. It is best described by Colossians 1:25-28.

²⁶ the mystery that has been kept hidden for ages and generations, but is now disclosed to the Lord's people. ²⁷ To them God has chosen to make known among the Gentiles the glorious riches of this mystery, which is Christ in you, the hope of glory.

²⁸ He is the one we proclaim, admonishing and teaching everyone with all wisdom, so that we may present everyone fully mature in Christ."

Dr. Nkansah is an author and Preacher to be watched and followed as his teachings of God's Word continue to break boundaries and reach many levels through his strikingly different ways of communicating the Word to the World.

Evelyn Botchway, MHA
Research Administrative Officer

INTRODUCTION

The only way to deal with situations in one's life that are beyond their control and still appear to be unfazed and in control is to have a continuous prayer habit to overcome those challenges spiritually and physically.

A person's solution to challenges must be their trade secret and a hidden weapon to ensure a successful life. God gave instructions to Moses to tell the Priest in Leviticus 6:8-13 to maintain a steady flaming fire on the altar all day and all night; it must not go out. Reference to fire in the Bible symbolizes the presence of God, prayers, and the Holy Spirit in the New Testament. The New Testament explains that prayer is man's way of communicating with God in a private setting and that prayer can take on many forms. When dealing with demons of a supernatural nature, it is not difficult to pray, but it can be challenging to comprehend why the demons do what they do.

To access the throne of God, the dimension that deals in the supernatural realm, requires various processes, forms, and directives. These can differ depending on the individual's prayer requests and the results sought. If you do not understand the rituals and procedures associated with spiritual practices, praying will be like entering a bedroom to have a mere conversation, which will be all there is to it, instead of having an intimate and a deep conversation with God.

THE PREPARATION OF YOUR HEART AND READINESS TO MEET WITH GOD BY FAITH IS ESSENTIAL TO START A SUCCESSFUL PRAYER.

Prayer must come out of a sincere heart, a heart ready to forgive and move on. In worshipping and praying to God, it is not only by might or power but by our readiness to allow the Spirit of the Living God to take over and use the soul, body, and Spirit as a channel to intercede on behalf of others on the throne of God. Faith plays an essential role in pleasing God, without faith, it is impossible to please Him. It is essential for those seeking God to believe that He is a reward for those who diligently seek Him. (Hebrews 11:6) To receive God's tips, we must think and know He is out there and ready to favor us abundantly. Remember, God, rewards those who seek him with all their hearts. The book of James described prayer as "the effectual fervent of the righteous man avails much." (James 5:16).

The Children of God would always get into the throne's deepest chambers and touch God's heart to move Him to improve their situations if all the conditions to access the Throne are present in one's prayer life and mastery. If those conditions exist in one's prayer life, favorable divine consideration would be the case. As a result, one must practice self-control for prayer to be effective. James described prayer as an actor capable of producing an

2

intended effect, having great warmth or intensity in the Spirit, feeling, or enthusiasm. The following lessons will cover some of the dimensions, protocols, and levels most associated with prayer practice.

Jesus said the only way to overcome the challenges of life and demonic attacks is through prayer and fasting. The act of praying is a form of active or powerful force used to exert pressure on the situation in question (Matthew 17:21). The New Living Translation says that a righteous person's earnest prayer has great power and produces incredible results. Amen

CHAPTER ONE

THE EFFECTS THAT PRAYER HAS AND THE POWERS IT HOLDS

Pray for healing for each other after you have confessed your trespasses. Righteous men can obtain much by praying fervently and effectively. (James 5:16).

1. No boundaries can restrict the power of prayer

2. There is no physical barrier that can prevent the effectiveness of prayer

3. The power of prayer does not discriminate against or limit individuals

4. The power of prayer could break through any barriers or limitations that stand in its way

The idea that someone who prays can acquire power for themselves through praying seems to be true. God's power motivates the activity of prayer, which attends to our supplications and answers them, according to the Bible. As a result, prayer determines the scope of the measures that God will take in response to the challenges that the children of God are confronting at the particular time.

The power of prayer does not come from them; What is the power of prayer? | GotQuestions.org. It is not the words they say, the way they tell them, or even how often they repeat them. Instead, the power of prayer comes from something beyond them. No one method or posture is superior to others regarding the efficacy of prayer. The use of antiques, icons, candles, or beads in worship does not impart any additional spiritual benefit. Prayers are effective only when they are heard and answered by the all-powerful One. Because prayer puts people in touch with the All-Powerful God, the person praying should anticipate receiving mighty answers to their prayers and requests, regardless of whether God decides to grant our petitions, or not. The God to whom people pray is the source of the power of prayer, and He can and will (What is the power of prayer? | GotQuestions.org) respond to them according to His perfect will and timing. That is true regardless of the response that God chooses to provide to our petitions.

1. NO BOUNDARIES CAN RESTRICT THE POWER OF PRAYER

The power of prayer transcends all boundaries; this implies that Prayer doesn't have limits, weaknesses, lack of capacity, inability, or handicaps that prevent it from working successfully against its targets.

Prayer is the only human medium of spiritual warfare.

Prayer is the only human channel of spiritual warfare, and the power of God can permeate all aspects of a person's life and can break through anything that hinders the resilience of peoples' petitions. God's word has a life and power that is sharper than any two-edged sword, and it penetrates even the dividing line between body and spirit, joints, and marrow, and discerns the thoughts and intents of the heart. (Hebrews 4:12).

The voices that speak for peace and serenity are those of individuals who believe in God. When people pray, they are not only expressing what is on their minds; in addition, via their prayers, they are exhibiting the power that God possesses and His presence

Prayer has the potential to destroy obstacles, fortifications, and citadels on any level of a person's life, be it the physical, the spiritual, the emotional, or the psychological. Once the act of praying has begun, it is impossible to set limitations and constraints or reverse the prayer itself. No single restriction may apply to undo the favorable circumstances that God has bestowed on a follower of Jesus Christ in this life.

Alternately, the invocation cannot be interrupted in any way, nor can it affect the target, and it cannot restrict the mark in any way. God is everywhere at once, allowing him to govern everything and listen to people's pleas from various locations and distances. It is possible that many individuals may be praying to the same God from different places at the same time and yet that God can listen to their prayers and locate them all based on what they are asking for at the same time.

Case studies from the Bible demonstrate the effectiveness of prayer

Sometimes, people prayed in the Bible to bring God's immediate attention to a particular circumstance so that He would help them. These prayers appear in the Bible. Despite this, the conditions under which they arise and the locations where they occur are typically incomprehensible to us.

Case Study 1 – The prayer that Jonah offered up while in the belly of the fish

Jonah 2:1-10

Jonah was a prophet of God tasked with warning the people of Nineveh of the repercussions of their misdeeds. However, when he disobeyed God and tried to void his commission, he was punished for his disobedience and ended up being swallowed by a large fish. While he was in the stomach of the fish, Jonah prayed to the same God he had disobeyed earlier to rescue him, saying: "

From inside the fish Jonah prayed to the Lord his God. ² He said:

> *"In my distress I called to the Lord,*
> *and he answered me.*
> *From deep in the realm of the dead I called for help,*
> *and you listened to my cry.*
> *³ You hurled me into the depths,*
> *into the very heart of the seas,*
> *and the currents swirled about me;*
> *all your waves and breakers*
> *swept over me.*

⁴ I said, 'I have been banished
from your sight;
yet I will look again
toward your holy temple.'
⁵ The engulfing waters threatened me,[b]
the deep surrounded me;
* seaweed was wrapped around my head.*

⁶ To the roots of the mountains I sank down;
the earth beneath barred me in forever.
But you, Lord my God,
brought my life up from the pit.

Please reach them through their precious temple, and the Lord came to mind just as our life was about to ebb away. Those who worship in vain idols, have given up on the possibility of steadfast love. However, in the Spirit of appreciation, the people of God will make a sacrifice for Him. They intend to keep their word and pay what they promised. Only the Lord saves!"

Jonah was cast ashore by the fish as an immediate response to the Lord's words. Stand and pray from a heart of repentance; regardless of where the problem originated, God is the same gracious, loving and kind being that He was yesterday, today, and forever; He will prove His sympathy and deliverance to them that seek his direction. Prayer will continue to demonstrate its effectiveness, despite our limitations. Sometimes those who love God find themselves in situations where they are helpless, desperate, and alone, and the only thing they can do is to reflect in prayer and on the Word of God in the hopes that God will intervene on their behalf.

Case Study 2 – The prayers of Shadrach, Meshach, and Abednego, with the fourth man in the burning fire

Daniel 3:17-27

People who pray need to maintain their composure, keep their attention focused on the task at hand, and behave themselves in a manner that is fitting for children of God, which means acting in a controlled manner that is free of fear and anxiety. Notwithstanding that, there is still a possibility that human beings will fall into temptations, either accidentally or on purpose. Yet, they must continue to pray until they experience a miracle to have any chance of succeeding.

Even though doing so would have resulted in their deaths in the blazing furnace, Shadrach, Meshach, and Abednego were adamant in their conviction that they would not turn their backs on the God of their forefathers. Although they were in a difficult situation, they reaffirmed their faith by saying, "Even if it comes to pass that our God will not save us, we will never bow down to the God of Nebuchadnezzar," which shows how strongly they felt about their faith.

After much deliberation, the three were finally cast carelessly into the blazing flames as a cruel prank. Even when the fire of death enveloped them and engulfed them, they continued to pray in the same manner as they always did. That proves the power of Prayer is all required during trying times when there is opposition and difficulties. Believe in the word of God, which declares that God will never leave or forsake those who are His children. That is a secure promise recorded in the Bible.

Nebuchadnezzar ordered them to enter the fiery furnace, which had reached a temperature seven times higher than it would have usually been. However, when the king turned to look, he saw four figures walking through the flames without being hurt, and the fourth of these figures appeared to be "like a son of God." When Nebuchadnezzar realized what was taking place, he rushed to rescue the youths and placed them in positions of authority. There was not even a whiff of smoke on their clothing when God revealed himself as their savior. That was a clear sign that God had saved them. He was the fourth man and will be there for you whenever you require his assistance in any location or circumstance. He will always be there for you.

The power of prayer can go through protocols in heaven, under the sun, and in every spirit realm. It goes beyond the sea, and prayer can penetrate the bones and marrow and cut through every vein to heal. "For the word of God is alive and active. Sharper than any double-edged sword, it penetrates even to dividing soul and spirit, joints and marrow; it judges the thoughts and attitudes of the heart." Hebrews 4:12 God's word is not only alive but also powerful.

Case Study 3 - Paul and Silas's Prayer in Jail

Another case study where we see prayer could not be limited or reduced by no means is about Paul and Silas in the Book of Acts of the Apostles 16:18-31. Paul and Silas were on their way to prayer, when they were accosted by a servant who had a spirit by which she predicted the future. She harassed them by following them over several days, calling out after them "these men are servants of the Most High God, who are telling you the way to be saved." Finally, in exasperation, Paul called out to the spirit, "Come out in the name of Jesus!" At that exact moment, the Spirit emerged departed from the girl. The girl's owners had made a good deal of money by fortune telling. After realizing their hope of profit was gone, they seized Paul and Silas and forced them to appear before the rulers in the marketplace. The magistrates ripped off their clothing and ordered them to be beaten with rods when they presented them to the magistrates, claiming, "These men are Jews who are causing trouble."

They advocate customs that Romans are forbidden to practice or accept. The crowd attacked them, and the magistrates ripped off their garments and gave them the order to beat them. Finally, after they had struck them hard, they threw them into prison, and asked the jailer to guard them carefully. The jailer followed their orders. Consequently, he locked their feet up in stocks and confined them in the inner prison.

The Philippian jailer convert.

They were singing hymns to God at midnight; and suddenly, there was a great earthquake, so the prison's foundations were shaking. Additionally, all the doors immediately opened, and the bonds on all of them immediately dissolved. The jailer found the prison doors open when he woke up and drew his sword kill himself if the prisoners had escaped. Then Paul shouted, "Do not hurt yourself, for we are all here." As the jailer ran towards Paul and Silas, shaking with fear, he fell before them. Afterward, he brought them out and asked, "Sirs, what do I have to do to be saved?" And they answered, "You and your household must believe in Jesus Christ."

God consistently demonstrates his power through fearful, faithful, and prayerful children of God. *The Supplications of God's people will never be in vain; therefore, they should continue praying until what they are hoping for comes to pass.*

2. THERE IS NO PHYSICAL BARRIER THAT CAN PREVENT THE EFFECTIVENESS OF PRAYER

Another way of putting it is the source of prayers. People can pray no matter their circumstances, location, or who they are with. Nehemiah prayed from a foreign land in Susa, the Citadel.

Case Study 4 – Nehemiah's prayer of the building of the Wall.

Nehemiah 1:4-11

He immediately began crying and mourning for several days while praying to the Lord when he first heard these words. After that, he addressed himself to "O my Lord, the great God in heaven. Those who love him and obey his precepts will benefit from the great and awesome God's continued love and fidelity to their covenant with him. Let his eyes and ears be open to hear the prayer that the people now make before him day and night for the people of Israel, confessing the sins that we have committed against our God, that we have sinned against Israel. " Even our father's household has been guilty of sin. We have been evil toward God, and we have disobeyed his commandments, statutes, and rules that he gave to Moses as his servant.

Keep in mind the instruction that God gave to Moses, his servant. "If they are unfaithful, he will scatter them among the peoples," the Bible says. However, if you turn back to me and obey my commandments, even if your disobedient children spread across the universe's farthest reaches, He will gather them and bring them to the dwelling place I have chosen for my name. " They are the servants of God and the people of God, whom God has redeemed through the great power and strong hand that he possesses. "May the ear of God be attentive to the prayer of both his servants and those who adore his name, and may God grant success to his servant today, and may God grant him mercy in his sight."

Nehemiah was a cupbearer to the king.

Nehemiah was a member of the Jewish exile, and was a cupbearer to the foreign king who held the Jews in exile. When he heard about the plight of the returnees to his country, he did not look down on allow his situation as a foreigner or a servant to the king to dampen his spirit. He began praying for a solution. It makes no difference whether the people praying are from another country or what nation they pray in because prayer is effective. Therefore, there needs to be immediate attention given to prayers wherever people are praying, and they should begin wherever necessary.

Simple Prayer Evidence – Nehemiah 2:1-5

While serving King Artaxerxes, the king became aware that something was amiss with the prophet. The king was curious as to the cause of Nehemiah's gloomy disposition. Nehemiah told the king about the desolation of Jerusalem, and his wish to rebuild parts of the city. According to verse 4b, the king responded: "If your servant wants to, you can let him rebuild the city in Judah where his ancestors rest.". That was a straightforward prayer request made without trepidation or doubt. What Nehemiah prayed for has just been granted by the king. That calls for the children of God to pray without hesitation in times of difficulties. Make it a habit to pray, and you might discover that God is holding you safe in his arms.

The principle of praying anywhere.

It is of the utmost importance that church ministers who only want members to come to them for prayer do not infringe upon people's rights to pray and ask for help on their own, as this would be a violation of those rights. It is also of the utmost importance that church ministers do not infringe upon people's rights to pray and ask for help on their own. That implies a suppression of the right to insistent asking without qualms. The Bible does not command us to ask for prayer from someone in a higher position in ministry, but tells us to pray to our God, Who longs to freely distribute to anyone who wishes to pray with the right attitude of good Spirit before Him.

Jesus encouraged us in Matthew 7:7 not to be timid in prayer but to "Ask, and you shall receive; seek, and you shall find; knock, and opportunity will come unto you: This implies insistent asking without qualms. Because Jesus did not instruct his disciples to pray in any location, the best place to begin praying is within oneself. That is because Jesus did not pray in any specific location, at any specific time, and with any particular or specific people.

3. THE POWER OF PRAYER DOES NOT DISCRIMINATE AGAINST OR LIMIT INDIVIDUALS

Considering that God is impartial, it follows that He listens to everyone regardless of their nationality, color, or background, whether rich or poor; God invites them all to the altar of prayer.

The God of deliverance has answered the blessings of the rich, poor, free, and bound. When Peter met with the gentile centurion Cornelius, he clarified that God cared not for the nation he came from, but that in every country, God accepted those who feared him and worked righteousness" (Acts 10:34-35, NKJV). The NKJV translates "God does not show partiality" as "God does not show favoritism."

Jews believed God loved them more than gentiles, but Peter understood that God did not treat them differently. God desires that people of all nations repent and be saved (2 Peter 3:9; 1 Timothy 2:4). In explaining the order of God's plan, the apostle Paul did not mean to indicate unfairness or favoritism. Every person who sins will suffer trouble and calamity, both Jews and Gentiles. Nevertheless, God will bring honor, glory, and peace to everyone who does good for both the Jew and Gentile. He favors no one over another" (Romans 2:9-11, New Living Translation).

God also forbids us from showing favoritism. James 2:9 says that "respect to persons" and "partiality" (NKJV) is sin. It is evident by considering the context of this passage in the New Living Translation: However, we must not show egoism in prayers but pray for all. "Brothers and sisters, how can you profess your faith in Jesus Christ if you favor some people more than others? For example, let us say someone comes dressed in fancy clothes and pricey jewelry, and another comes dressed in worn clothes and wearing no jewelry. People give special attention and a good seat to the rich, but they say to the poor, 'They can stand over there, or else sit on the floor well. Doesn't this discrimination show that wrong motives guide us? ...

16

"Yes indeed, it is good to truly obey our Lord's royal command found in the Scriptures: 'Love your neighbor as yourself.' Nevertheless, if they pay special attention to the rich, they sin, for they are guilty of breaking that law" (James 2:1-4, 8-9). Therefore, God shows no favoritism or partiality, and the Bible teaches us that we should not either. When it comes to Prayer, God listened to every human being who avails themselves as a vessel for God to use. Indeed, God could use anything how much more than His image.

Jesus taught us that God is our heavenly Father, so we should be able to go to Him in boldness and confidence for all our needs. Children must be able to speak to their fathers directly for their own needs. They do not always tell one of their siblings to go for their school fees and ask for other necessities from their father. A father's responsibility is to listen to and care for all his children, regardless of their needs. God loves everyone; equally. Even the gentile centurion Cornelius's prayers were answered and moved God to send Peter in response to his prayer. " although he was a gentile."

4. THE POWER OF PRAYER COULD BREAK THROUGH ANY BARRIERS OR LIMITATIONS THAT STAND IN ITS WAY

When one shares space with a hostile neighbor, even a flower growing over their fence could lead to an altercation. It always seems that there is an invisible line that one may not cross. It gives the impression that if you cross the line your neighbor has drawn, he will become hostile toward you, and it will be your fault! Trying to counter that may appear like hitting one's head against a rock. Or one could follow the advice given in Proverbs 26:4, which states, "Do not answer a fool according to his folly, lest you become like him yourself."

(ref). Knock when turning steering wheel | Saabscene Saab Forum - Saab ....

However, prayer has a substance that has the potential to impact circumstances beyond the regions controlled by the enemy in a way that is favorable to the person praying.

As a result, the power of prayer monitors the area that the adversary controls and demonstrates its strength over the operative demons when people are praying.

A prayer that is effective, heartfelt, and goes beyond the bounds of possibility may be that of a rescue operation team consisting of military personnel to rescue victims from kidnappers. It's incredible how much strength it has behind it.

CHAPTER TWO

THREE STRATEGIES FOR PRAYER THAT WORKS EFFECTIVE

For we might become the righteousness of God in him, he who knew no sin became sin for us. 2 Corinthians 5:21

1. Prayer is effective in conjunction with a moral life and righteousness

2. Praying makes prayers effective through the development of faith.

3. Prayers are effective when we obey God.

1. PRAYER IS EFFECTIVE IN CONJUNCTION WITH A MORAL LIFE AND RIGHTEOUSNESS

In his body, Jesus took the punishment for our sins and died for us; since he did so, the Bible allows us to forget all our sins so that we can ignore both ours and Jesus' sins. Therefore, we owe nothing to anyone but our continuing obligation to love one another. Anyone who loves their neighbor as themselves fully satisfies the

19

requirements of the law. (Romans 13:8). Jesus explained what righteousness means to him in John 1:29. Jesus came toward John, and he shouted, "Behold! The Lamb of God who takes away our sins!" The only person and means to completely take the world's sins are Jesus Christ and the power of his blood. Righteousness occurs when a person has fully atoned for their sins.

Righteousness plays an essential role in prayer. God wants us to stand before him and communicate with Him by standing clothed in righteousness. In this way, he made the One without sin the sin for us, and by His righteousness, we might become as honest as He is. 2 Corinthians 5:21. A righteous man's prayer is filled with confidence and boldness. When one harbors sin, his prayer will be feeble and will not achieve its aim. Children of God certainly feel more confident in prayer when they live a righteous life before God. Jesus Christ proved His righteous life against the devil by saying he would no longer talk much with them, "For the ruler of this world is coming, and he has nothing in me. Brothers must have nothing against their fellow brothers when they stand in prayer. Confess, renounce, and denounce every known and unknown sin.

Nevertheless, we can share fellowship as a family if we walk in the light, and Christ's blood cleanses us of all sin. The truth is not in them, and those who claim to have no sin are lying to themselves, and the truth is not in them. The Lord forgives our sins and purifies us from unrighteousness if we confess them in faith. (1 John 1:7-9 N J V).

The believer of Jesus Christ must live a life beyond reproach: righteous living. At the same time, they must take a position to understand that Jesus died to put believers in righteousness. Thus, let us boldly approach the throne of grace so that we can find mercy and help in times of need. Hebrews 4:16. Jesus Christ exchanged his righteous position for humanity's sinful nature. He did all for us to communicate directly with the Father in heaven. They do not have to wait for any person or allow sin to hinder them from God. The people who confess Jesus as their Lord and Savior are at peace with God. There is no condemnation for those that are in Christ Jesus. Romans 8:1-2.

Righteousness is a defensive weapon against the devil and his host. When people believe and live righteously, they could stand anywhere boldly in prayer.

Therefore, stand firm, children of God girded with truth by the waist and breastplate of righteousness on Ephesians 6:13-17. In Ephesians 6, Paul talks about the breastplate of righteousness as the second piece of the armor of God. To be righteous means obeying God's commandments and living in an honorable way to Him. Psalm 106:3 says, "How blessed are those who keep justice, who practice righteousness at all times!". Here, we are using the armor and battle dress of the Roman soldier of the first century as a metaphor. Still following the military metaphor, we are in the middle of a war. As a result, we should never quench the Spirit and keep the praying Spirit without ceasing.

Personal faith that positions itself against evil and aggressive prayer warfare that assails demonic strongholds are two distinct and complementary facets of spiritual life. 1 Thessalonians 5:17,19. Wearing the breastplate of righteousness, all spiritual warfare is victorious only based upon using the cross and the blood of Christ (Colossians 2:15). Righteousness is the powerful force that energizes spiritual warfare for Christian a victorious Christian life. Believers should live a victorious life of righteousness supported by divine power in prayers.

A prayer offered by a righteous man to the Lord God Almighty is powerful enough to overcome any obstacle, and the presence of righteousness poses a danger to the demonic stronghold. The act of praying is a stage of warfare, and as such, it requires all the appropriate army dress code. According to Ephesians 6:14, righteousness must wear the armor of God to win the battle.

Christianity differs significantly from other religions.

Christ, the Holy Son of God, took on the guilt of sinful people and died in our stead to bring about reconciliation between God and people who are by our nature sinful.. Because Jesus Christ went to the cross in their place to take their punishment so that all people could be set free from the threat of execution, God pardoned us and declared us to be righteous.

In addition, not only does He forgive us for our sins, but He also credits us with the righteous actions of His Son. That was an incredible display of graciousness. We acknowledge that Christ's perfect righteousness before God was sufficient to cover our sins and the weight of our guilt. Christ's sacrifice on the cross atones for all our sins; in return, we receive his spotless righteousness. He sacrificed His holiness to pay for the sins of men.

We have all of this because of God, who reconciled us through Christ and gave us the ministry of reconciliation" (2 Corinthians 5:18). The word "Reconciliation" comes from the Latin word

"Reconciliāre", meaning "to make good again" or "to repair." In the original translation, "reconciles" refers to converting coins, changing money, then individuals changing and believing. In one another." "For if through His death, we were enemies, much more, through His reconciliation, we have salvation" (Romans 5:10). God's love provided a means and foundation for man's reconciliation to the One he had offended. God's sense of justice must be satisfied (Rom. 3:26). We deserve the wrath of God. Therefore, God gave His Son a propitiation for our sins (Rom. 3:25; Col. 1:20; 1 John 2:2; 4:10). God turns away His wrath in response to the sacrifice of His Son for the believer. God needs no reconciliation; we are the ones who need reconciling to Him. We are the sinning rebels. God makes this possible through Christ's death.

Two significant scripture passages present the heart of the Good News of Jesus Christ. Bible guides and commentaries are also instrumental in explaining the complicated, hard-to-understand passages. "All glory to God, because Christ, the only begotten son of the Father, gave Himself up for the world, so anyone who believes in Him will not perish, but have eternal life" (John 3:16). God demonstrated "His righteousness at this present time to prove that He is just and that faith in Jesus is the means to righteousness" (Romans 3:26). God cannot justify the sinner because He is holy and righteous. What is the purpose of justifying guilty sinners when God is holy and righteous? Or, to state it another way, how can a person be right with God?

The basis of our Christian life is the atonement of Jesus Christ and the imputation of the perfect righteousness of Christ to the believing sinner. The apostle Paul told us how God did it. "He

[God] made Him [Jesus Christ] our sin so that through Him we might become the righteousness of God" (2 Corinthians 5:21). Note the contrast and results in this great verse. God made Him so that Him [Jesus Christ] who knew no sin might become sin for sinners so that we sinners become the righteousness of God on our behalf in Him.

God is responsible for our eternal salvation, namely, that by Jesus Christ, He reconciled the world to Himself without counting our sins against us. He has conveyed the word of reconciliation to us. (2 Corinthians 5:19). God performed a double transfer of power. Christ took on Himself our sins and credited us with His perfect righteousness. In this book, we can forget all our sins. As a result, He took our sins and put them on Himself, so we do not have to pay for them. It was our punishment, and He died in our place. The righteousness of Christ owes his existence to us, believing sinners, so that he might accept us. God acquits the guilty sinner who believes in the atoning sacrifice of Jesus Christ for his sins.

Bible verses about righteousness.

"I put on righteousness as my clothing; justice was my robe and my turban.." — **Job 29:14**

"Fine linen, bright and clean, was given her to wear." — **Revelation 19:8**

"I delight greatly in the Lord; my soul rejoices in my God. For he has clothed me with garments of salvation and arrayed me in a robe of his righteousness, as a bridegroom adorns his head like a priest, and as a bride adorns herself with her jewels." — **Isaiah 61:10**

"He put on righteousness as his breastplate, and the helmet of salvation on his head; he put on the garments of vengeance and wrapped himself in zeal as in a cloak." — **Isaiah 59:17**

"Righteousness will be his belt and faithfulness the sash around his waist." — **Isaiah 11:5**

"All of us have become like one who is unclean, and all our righteous acts are like filthy rags; we all shrivel up like a leaf, and like the wind our sins sweep us away." — **Isaiah 64:6**

"May your priests be clothed with your righteousness; may your faithful people sing for joy." — **Psalm 132:9**

'The angel said to those who were standing before him, "Take off his filthy clothes. Then he said to Joshua, "See, I have taken away your sin, and I will put fine garments on you."' — **Zechariah 3:4**

"Yet you have a few people in Sardis who have not soiled their clothes. They will walk with me, dressed in white, for they are worthy." — **Revelation 3:4**

2. PRAYING BECOMES EFFECTIVE THROUGH THE DEVELOPMENT OF FAITH.

Faith is the bedrock of all miracles in prayer and grows like a mustard seed. There is such a thing as cooperation or community unbelief that prevented Christ from working. One of the reasons why Jesus appoints teachers is to enable them to deal with suspicion. During Jesus' boyhood and maturity in his hometown city of Nazareth, "he could not do mighty works there, because of their corporate unbelief." (Mark 6:5). The next episode

25

following this statement is that; "Jesus went about their villages teaching" Why? Because teaching is the antidote for unbelief to release the power of miracles in prayer.

We do not love people out of unbelief; we teach them out of it. Today's Christians depend on people praying for them, which modern attitude has given more preeminence to false prophets who deceive believers. We need to learn how to pray with faith that can move mountains and pray with faith already within us, pray with faith that grows significantly, and pray consistently and continuously to increase our faith. When Jesus talks about faith and prayer, they are always linked with our relationships with other people. If our faith is going to grow, it involves our relationship with other believers. Jesus teaches the disciples the following:

1. "So watch yourselves. If your brother or sister sins against you, rebuke them; and if they repent, forgive them. ⁴Even if they sin against you seven times in a day and seven times come back to you saying 'I repent,' you must forgive them." (Luke 17:3-4)

2. "And when you stand praying, if you hold anything against anyone, forgive them, so that your Father in heaven may forgive you your sins." (Mark 11:25)

3. ²³ "Therefore, if you are offering your gift at the altar and there remember that your brother or sister has something against you, ²⁴ leave your gift there in front of the altar. First go and be reconciled to them; then come and offer your gift. (Matthew 5:23-24)

In response to this teaching on forgiveness and human relationships, the apostles entreated the Lord to increase their faith. 'The apostles said to the Lord, "Increase our faith!"' (Luke 17:5). Prayer works, but it takes faith.

Faith in prayer grows in stages.

The next verse, Luke 17:6, is a shocking and the most misunderstood scripture of faith and prayer in the Bible. " He replied, "If you have faith as small as a mustard seed, you can say to this mulberry tree, 'Be uprooted and planted in the sea,' and it will obey you. The comparative passage in Mark 11:23 mentions not only trees but mountains. " "Truly I tell you, if anyone says to this mountain, 'Go, throw yourself into the sea,' and does not doubt in their heart but believes that what they say will happen, it will be done for them. The key is to believe in their own words and pray for themselves rather than someone else praying for them.

Not all of us can rearrange the topography (move mountains), so we have "spiritualized" this concept of mountain-moving faith idea. When we cannot make a scripture work, we "spiritualize" it, bringing God's Word down to our experience of God's Word. God wants His Word to work, and He wants our word to work. He says in Jeremiah 1:12. It is the will of God to conduct His word, and we need to find this kind of faith in "prayer that speaks," and then things will happen. Anytime and anywhere, God's children can demonstrate their faith in prayer. Now, back to Luke 17:6, which the Bible's expositors have interpreted thus: "it just takes a little bit of faith to make a big difference." The problem with this kind of doctrine is this; It does not work. No "Little" faith has ever accomplished "big" things.

The mustard seed faith

Their faith would grow like a grain of mustard seed. When children of God read that, the Spirit caused them to understand Jesus' teaching differently. The Lord Jesus was not telling them that all they need is a little faith, like a mustard seed, and then they can move mountains; instead, God was telling them that faith that GROWS as a mustard seed can heal the sick, cast out demons, and see signs as a result (Mark16:17-20). They have a divine commentary on how a grain of mustard see grows in Matthew 13:31, 32. The Lord's own words says: Another parable put him to them, saying, "Have you ever seen what someone plants in his field? Even though mustard seeds are tiny, they grow into huge plants that are incredibly powerful. Furthermore, it becomes a tree, so the air birds come and lodge in the branches thereof."

Although mustard seeds are tiny, Jesus said that once grown, they become the most significant herb, capable of growing large enough to shelter birds. Little faith will do some things, and immense faith will do bigger things, but faith that grows is essential. People progress toward ultimate, mature faith from "faith to faith" (Romans 1:17).

3. PRAYERS ARE EFFECTIVE WHEN WE OBEY GOD.

Obedience is the act or practice of acting on simple instructions. In 1 Thessalonians 5:17, the Apostle Paul gave simple instructions on prayer; thus, "pray continually". When the people bring their gifts to the altar and then remember that they have something against someone else, they should leave their gifts there in front of the altar and then go on their way to make peace with their neighbor first before returning to bring their gifts. Before making an offering, those who are God's children must obey instructions as straightforward as the one given above. People cannot talk about being obedient to simple instructions and leave the character of Saul out of the conversation. And Samuel said,

> *"Does the Lord delight in burnt offerings and sacrifices as much as in obeying the Lord? To obey is better than sacrifice, and to heed is better than the fat of rams. 23 For rebellion is like the sin of divination, and arrogance like the evil of idolatry. Because you have rejected the word of the Lord, he has rejected you as king." (1 Samuel 15:22,23)*

Disobedience is a branch of witchcraft that should never exist among Christians. God had promised us that He would stand behind His word to make it work. Our words in prayer are the direct word of the Holy Spirit. "…The Spirit helps us in our weakness. We do not know what we ought to pray for, but the Spirit himself intercedes for us through wordless groans. 27 And he who searches our hearts knows the mind of the Spirit, because the Spirit intercedes for God's people in accordance with the will of God." (Romans 8:26-27). Ceasing to pray is a dangerous trap of hidden temptation, and every child of God should heed the voice to pray anytime, anywhere, whenever prompted. It is unnecessary to deal with many of Satan's and his demons' afflictions if people obey and pray according to God's instructions. "Watch and pray so that you will not fall into temptation. The spirit is willing, but the flesh is weak." (Matthew 26:41). The key is watching and praying, so one does not fall prey to temptation. The devil and his demons will make believers worry or occupy them with distractions, but the Lord will not forsake His people, and before they call, He will answer them.

Moreover, while they are still speaking, God will hear. (Isaiah 65:24). Prayer is just the act of committing and submitting a request to God without hesitating or doubting.

CHAPTER THREE

THE CHARACTERS OF PRAYER

Human beings possess a spiritual creation in God's image, and everything around them is in two dimensions, spiritual and physical. Mostly, humans know of the material things but not the spiritual things.

The Holy Spirit of God has insight into mystical matters. Children are incapable of engaging in a spiritual conflict in the physical world and must instead pray to deal with spiritual issues. For them to be able to follow the correct procedures during worship, they will first need to realize that devotion is a spiritual act.

1. THE SPIRITUALITY OF PRAYER

Because humans are spirit beings, the beginning of their prayers should always direct them toward the Spirit. What matters most is not where someone worships but rather the state of one's heart and mind. The true meaning of prayer is not simply an act of ritual or ceremony but rather a spiritual reality that is congruent with the character of God as a Spirit. " God is spirit, and his worshipers must worship in the Spirit and in truth." (John 4:24). Now the Lord is the Spirit, and where the Spirit of the Lord is, there is freedom. (2 Corinthians 3:17)

2. NOT AGAINST FLESH AND BLOOD

The command to "finally" do something found in Ephesians 6:10 implies not in conclusion but insofar as changes to the rest of life are a concern. The ability to differentiate between the spiritual struggle and other social, personal, and political challenges is one of the most demanding requirements placed on Christians by the world's churches. Otherwise, individual believers and groups become far too easily sidetracked, "wrestling" with human adversaries rather than praying against the unseen works of hell operating in the background.

Indeed, "for our struggle is not against flesh and blood, but against the rulers, against the authorities, against the powers of this dark world and against the spiritual forces of evil in the heavenly realms.". (Ephesians 6:12). Earlier references to Spiritual resources available to the church (Ephesians 1:3). Christ's Authority over Satan (Ephesians 1:21). The church sits with her ascended Lord. The Father's will to display His wisdom through the church to the confounding of evil powers. (Ephesians 3:10). On the grounds, the passages announce the church's corporate assignment to prayer warfare so that God will advance and prevail in the world.

The life of humans is more spiritual than physical. Therefore, we must first enter the spiritual realm to inquire about everything we do in the form of prayer before we tackle it physically. At the beginning of creation, God used the dust of the earth to form man. It was still lifeless until God breathed into the dust image. Then the Bible says that man became a living soul. Man is clay and cannot do anything without being in the Spirit.

The Lord God formed man from the dust of the ground and breathed life into him, making him a living creature. (Genesis 2:7). Man was, in the beginning, doing everything spiritually until he sinned against God and translated to see everything physically when Adam transitioned from the garden to the land outside, separated, and self-dependent.

The Lord God said, " And the Lord God said, "The man has now become like one of us, knowing good and evil. He must not be allowed to reach out his hand and take also from the tree of life and eat, and live forever." So the Lord God banished him from the Garden of Eden to work the ground from which he had been taken. After he drove the man out, he placed on the east side of the Garden of Eden cherubim and a flaming sword flashing back and forth to guard the way to the tree of life." (Genesis 3:22-24)

3. THE INTENSITY OF PRAYER

We understand the Bible verse, "Not by might nor by power, but by My Spirit," says the Lord of hosts. (Zechariah 4:6) Moreover, we cannot override it, yet we also understand that prayer must be intense. Great energy, strength, concentration, and intensity should be the feeling power of their prayer. They should raise the temperature of prayer to a higher or an extreme degree as cold or heat. Jesus Christ suffered hemosiderosis (an overload of iron in the organs or tissues) while praying in the garden of Gethsemane before his crucifixion, as mentioned in the Defenders Bible by Physician Luke. That occurred after having supernatural encounters with God after one or two hours, persistent prayers that change circumstances, words in worship, dimension, direction, and spiritually leading.

"Elijah was a human being, even as we are. He prayed earnestly that it would not rain, and it did not rain on the land for three and a half years." (James 5:16-17). James described the prayer of prophet Elijah as Efficacious or effectual - Meaning; producing or able to produce the desired effect. Fervent prayer – extremely hot, to exhibiting or marked by great intensity of Spirit or feeling, enthusiasm, etc. Here is him praying.

To sum up, Elijah's prayers instruct the children of God that Prayer is to be operative, to be at work, and to put forth power in prayer. Prayer is a serious matter with God, and no one should take it lightly. It is necessary to punch the opponent powerfully to defeat him spiritually and physically.

4. THE RITUAL OF PRAYER

A ritual consists of actions, gestures, or words performed according to a particular pattern. In the raising of the son of the woman of Shunem when Elisha came into the house, the child lay dead in his bed. He went in, therefore, shut the door behind the two of them, and prayed to the Lord. Furthermore, the man of God went up and lay on the child, put his mouth on his mouth, eyes on his eyes, and hands-on his hands; and stretched himself out on the child, and the child's flesh became warm. He walked back and forth and stretched himself out on him again; the child sneezed seven times, then opened his eyes. Moreover, he called Gehazi and said, "Call this Shunammite woman." So, he called her. Moreover, when she came to him, he said, "Pick

34

up your son." So, she fell at his feet and bowed to the ground; then, she picked up her son and went out. (2 Kings 4: 32-37)

According to Elisha's story, prayer rituals look more like a picture than a description. During prayer, the Holy Spirit always directs what kind of ritual to perform according to the situation. Traditions within a religious community may prescribe rituals. Typical ritual characteristics include formality, traditionalism, invariance, governance by rules, and sacral symbolism. In all known human societies, rituals play a significant role. As well as rites and sacraments of organized religions and cults, the collection includes passage rites, atonement rites, dedication ceremonies, coronations, presidential inaugurations, weddings, and funerals. Even everyday actions like handshaking and saying "hello" may be rituals.

What does Acts chapter 16 mean? The field of ritual studies has seen conflicting definitions of the term. According to Kyriakos, ritual serves as an external or "etic" term for an action (or set of actions) that, from an outside perspective, appears irrational, incongruous, or contradictory. Similarly, insiders or "enemies" can use this term to acknowledge that non-initiated observers can perceive it. In a technical sense, ritual can refer to repetitive behavior used by individuals to cope. There is a connection to obsessive-compulsive behavior; however, obsessive-compulsive ritualistic behaviors tend to be isolated. The ritual in prayer referred to Mumming. (Mumming is a type of play where the participants act out a series of scenes in which a person is killed and then brought back to life by a doctor using a magic potion). The act of pretending to raise the dead through the use of some sort of magic potion violates the Christian doctrine and is considered blasphemy. Pretending to take on the powers of God has always been seen as blasphemy.

5. THE FIRE OF PRAYER

It is necessary to keep a constant fire burning in prayer to keep one's spiritual health alive and to remain in a continuous connection with the Maker to fulfill the requirements of the spirit, the soul, and the body.

The fire of love God ignited in the believer during the new birth must grow systematically to a higher degree of temperature.

"Once safely on shore, we found out that the island was called Malta. ² The islanders showed us unusual kindness. They built a fire and welcomed us all because it was raining and cold". ³ Paul gathered a pile of brushwood and, as he put it on the fire, a viper, driven out by the heat, fastened itself on his hand. ⁴ When the islanders saw the snake hanging from his hand, they said to each other, "This man must be a murderer; for though he escaped from the sea, the goddess Justice has not allowed him to live." ⁵ But Paul shook the snake off into the fire and suffered no ill effects. ⁶ The people expected him to swell up or suddenly fall dead; but after waiting a long time and seeing nothing unusual happen to him, they changed their minds and said he was a god." (Acts 28:3-6)

The viper emerged from the heat after Paul gathered a bundle of sticks and placed them on the fire. Do not leave the fire too cold or cool down when refining gold. The Dore must go through a trial by fire at a refinery. In an exciting process called refining, it is re-liquefied in a furnace and then heaped with generous amounts of soda ash and borax. This process then purifies the gold separating it from impurities

While everyone was busy helping in the crisis, the apostle gathered a bundle of sticks suitable for the fire and did not consider such an act beneath him. He was humble and not condescending. He and laid the wood on the fire, meaning to increase it. There came a viper out of the heat. *Acts 28:3 - KJV - And when Paul had gathered a bundle of sticks, and ....*

Viper Snake Facts

Vipers are among the most dangerous snakes.

A viper has a stocky body, and a large head,

Vipers have long, hinged fangs for injecting venom in the front of its mouth.

The venom causes a serious and potentially lethal wound.

Vipers hunt warm-blooded prey including rats and mice.

Some vipers hunt during the day, while are usually active at night.

They have two heat-sensitive pits between their eyes and mouth for sensing a prey's body heat.

The majority of vipers can be found in the tropics, but some can also be found in colder climates.

Most vipers, unlike other snakes are viviparous, giving birth to live young.

Furthermore, the snake's snout is similar in length to a hog's snout and has sixteen immovable teeth in each jaw and two large, hollow, sharp, hook-shaped, transparent canines on either side of its upper jaw. Those that cause mischief are flexible in their articulation, laid flat across the jaw, the animal never raising them except when it bites. These teeth, or fangs, have roots covered with a cyst or bladder, containing a large amount of substance drop of a yellow insipid saliva's juice. The snake has only one row of teeth, whereas other serpents have two; it is not fetid, whereas other serpents' interiors are intolerable. This serpent creeps very slowly and never leaps, though it can bite when provoked.

The bite of this snake is terrifying, and the poison of its taste is hazardous. Vipers have enzymatic venom that affects a wide variety of tissues. It induces extreme swelling, discomfort, and necrosis, or the death and decay of cells. It also has anticoagulant properties. A sudden decrease in blood pressure normally results in death. viper bites require immediate medical attention. There are two colors to its body, ash-colored or yellow, and its ground has spots of brownish color; under its belly are scales that are polished steel in color. In the Syriac translation, it says, "there came out of them (the sticks) a viper, forced by the heat of the fire"; it had lain silently among the posts, where this creature often lies, but when the fire got hot, it sprang out of them and fastened on his hand.

During prayers for deliverance, the demons in a person's body cannot continue to reside there, so they begin to manifest and leave the person. The type of demon that manifested itself as a viper when the fire was getting hotter was the kind of demon that could appear during believers' effectual and fervent prayer.

CHAPTER FOUR

WE ARE KINGDOM OF PRIESTS

*A priest is authorized to perform the sacred rites (Prayer),
especially as a mediatory agent between humans and God.*

God had complete sway in all things since all the Earth was His. Exodus 19:5. In His Kingdom, His submissive, Royal priests would rule over the planet in perpetuity, Amen.

In Ezekiel 22:30, the prophet speaks on God's behalf when he says, "I searched for somebody to build the wall and fill the gap for me on behalf of the land so that I wouldn't have to destroy it. But I was unable to locate anyone." In the situation described above, to expose oneself to defend something, to take the place of a fallen defender or supporter, or to protect against any advancing threat, implies filling the gap.

God searched for someone to "stand in the gap" *STRANGERS + EXILES: STANDING IN THE GAP* and be an advocate for the people in verse 30 above, but He was unable to find anybody. Thus, He concludes his declaration by pronouncing guilt and a threat of wrath. People's incapacity to make themselves available to intercede will always cause God's wrath towards humanity, particularly in their present state of sin.

1. EVERYONE IS APPOINTED A PRIEST TO PRAY

It seems fitting that the priesthood's role in mediation should serve as an invitation to the children of God to pray, as stated in the scriptures. Therefore, whenever folks stopped praying, God ceased to work for them. As a result, everyone should persistently pray to God to act in their favor because it is in their power to serve as intercessors.

Those who do not pray cannot complete the assignment that comes with this world because of its significance. Prayer is necessary to gain the strength to fulfill this responsibility in life. They can never pray for people not joining to become stars, which is one thing they can never do. They have the beautiful ability to dance from morning until night, but prayer is not part of their culture or tradition, so they will not be able to pray, they may have the beautiful ability to dance from morning until night, but prayer is not their calling.

They are unable to engage in spiritual conflict if they do not pray. People do not engage in sexual activity for any reason other than their desire to. They rebel against God and engage in sexual sin as a direct result of the territorial spirit fostered within them by the prince responsible for their captivity. Therefore, before preaching to those princes, they need to first engage in spiritual and prayer warfare with them.

Jesus saw Satan fall like lightning from heaven. It was by the strength of that engagement in prayer against the demonic forces to descend from heaven. (Luke 10:18). Daniel said, "I Daniel, I understood by books that the captivity of Israel should be 70 years, but he went on his knees and said for 21 days I ate no peaceable bread; as he was praying, the Angel Gabriel showed up. Then the angel said to Daniel, "Do not fear, Daniel, for, from the first day when you chose to understand and humble yourself before your God, He heard you, and I have come to you because of your words. Despite holding out for 21 days against God's servant, one of the chief princes, Michael, came to his aid, for there was no one to assist him there with the kings of Persia. Now he has come to make them understand what will happen to their people on the last day. The vision points to many days yet to come." (Daniel 10:12-14) Exodus 12:12 "I will judge gods of Egypt.

People pray for this reason, and they need to start translating spiritual things into material things for their benefit so they can make use of them. People pray because if they do not, they won't be able to benefit from or use the things in the Spirit to make those things real for them in the physical world. Therefore, people must pray persistently and consistently.

2. JESUS CHRIST IS OUR PERFECT EXAMPLE OF PRIESTHOOD AND AN INTERCESSOR.

While he was in excruciating pain, he prayed even for those who were responsible for his death. While Jesus was in agony, he absolved them of their sins and prayed for them. Because they were oblivious of the consequences of their actions, Father forgave

41

them. (Luke 23:34) It is difficult to ignore the transgressions of another person unless others around them are constantly nosy like the master was. The only way to keep a generation from committing sin and teaching them to live righteous lives is to actively involve them in prayer and instruct them in the word of God.

It is not that people do not have a high priest above their problems, instead they have one who is like them but without sin. (Hebrews 4:13). Jesus knows what they feel and go through. Christ Jesus, who died and rose from the dead, who now sits at God's right hand, intercedes on behalf of His people. This intercession resonates with John 17:22, which refers to the "heavenly communion" between Christ and God the Father. (Hebrews 7:25).

3. NINE BIBLE VERSES ABOUT THE KINGDOM OF PRIESTS

1. **Isaiah 61:6.** "And you will be called priests of the Lord, you will be named ministers of our God. You will feed on the wealth of nations, and in their riches you will boast."

2. **Isaiah 66:21.** "And I will select some of them also to be priests and Levites," says the Lord.

3. **Exodus 19:6.** "You will be for me a kingdom of priests and a holy nation.' These are the words you are to speak to the Israelites."

4. **Revelation 1:6** "And has made us to be a kingdom and priests to serve his God and Father—to him be glory and power for ever and ever! Amen."

5. **Revelation 5:10** "You have made them to be a kingdom and priests to serve our God, and they will reign on the earth."

6. **1 Peter 2:9** "But you are a chosen people, a royal priesthood, a holy nation, God's special possession, that you may declare the praises of him who called you out of darkness into his wonderful light."

7. **1 Peter 2:5**. Through Jesus Christ, believers become a spiritual house that offers spiritual sacrifices acceptable to God "You also, like living stones, are being built into a spiritual house to be a holy priesthood, offering spiritual sacrifices acceptable to God through Jesus Christ."

8. **Revelation 20:6.** "Blessed and holy are those who share in the first resurrection. The second death has no power over them, but they will be priests of God and of Christ and will reign with him for a thousand years."

9. **Romans 15:16.** "To be a minister of Christ Jesus to the Gentiles. He gave me the priestly duty of proclaiming the gospel of God, so that the Gentiles might become an offering acceptable to God, sanctified by the Holy Spirit."

4. CONFRONTING OBSTACLES WITH SILENCE AND TRUST IN GOD THROUGH PRAYER AND MEDITATION

When people pray to God about a particular matter, they do not speak about the issue, discuss it, worry about it, or complain about it. Instead, they thank God for it in obedience, humility, patience, and hope, waiting for whatever they desire. That is the proper way to maintain silence while praying for success.

In this way, people credit God for answering their prayers and acknowledge that the answer comes not from human might or power but from the Holy Spirit of the Lord. (Zechariah 4:6)

When individuals place their confidence in God, there are times when they should keep their mouths shut and not make any excuses for themselves. One such occasion is when believers are targeted with rumors. Because rumors are untrue, the truth will eventually disprove them. When Nehemiah was accused falsely on several occasions, instead of defending himself, he decided to keep silent and give the matter into God's care.

In Jesus' sham trial the chief priests and council tried to find false testimony against Jesus that would lead to His death. They could not find any, even though false witnesses had come forward. However, later, two people came forward and stated, "That man stated he was capable of destroying the temple of God and rebuilding it within three days." "Then the high priest stood up and said to Jesus, "Are you not going to answer? What is this testimony that these men are bringing against you?" [63] But Jesus remained silent."

Despite his silence, the high priest questioned Him, The high priest said to him, "I charge you under oath by the living God: Tell us if you are the Messiah, the Son of God." Jesus responded, saying, "You have said so," Jesus replied. "But I say to all of you: From now on you will see the Son of Man sitting at the right hand of the Mighty One and coming on the clouds of heaven." Matthew 26:59–64

When making decisions, there are times when it reaches a point where there must be complete silence to reflect and keep the information hidden from the adversary while prayer is taking place. The spiritual power of silence is immense, and this force brings down Satan's kingdom.

Most people keep their plans and objectives to themselves rather than discussing them with others, which is understandable given that this is how life works. It is possible to give the best answer to prayer by working in silence and allowing the results to speak for themselves. That is a terrific option.

In some situations, the more people we talk about what we are doing, the more likely it is that we will fail and fall, becoming victims of forces that are working against us of which we are unaware.

It is even possible that our friends do not support our goals and wish they never come true, but if people keep their prayers to God alone, it is easier to reach the results they seek.

One's conscience, as in I would love to go, but a still small voice tells me I must stay home and work. The expression appears in the Bible (1 Kings 19:12), in which Elijah hears his inner voice. Then a fire followed the earthquake, but the Lord did not appear, and a still, small voice appeared after the fire." Silence is a way of humbleness and surrender. It does not mean defeat, or you cannot do it. That means taking time off to focus on God and getting to know his ways. If only people would let God into their lives and their circumstances, he is ready and able to do so many beautiful things in those lives.

Moses said to Joshua during exaltation. "Keep this Book of the Law always on your lips; meditate on it day and night, so that you may be careful to do everything written in it. Then you will be prosperous and successful. 9 Have I not commanded you? Be strong and courageous. Do not be afraid; do not be discouraged, for the Lord your God will be with you wherever you go." Joshua 1:8-9. Children of God need to break from prayers and get back to God to hear what He must tell them. However, it's important to remember that prayer isn't just talking to God; it also involves silent meditation and reading the Bible in silence.

Scripture tells us that silence can help us avoid sinning (Proverbs 10:19), gain respect (Proverbs 11:12), and appear wise and intelligent (Proverbs 17:28). In other words, you may be blessed by holding your tongue. Ultimately, refraining from speaking in certain situations means we are practicing self-control. Even fools are thought wise if they keep silent, and discerning if they hold their tongues. (Proverbs 17:28)

God believes His children are intelligent, and if they do his bidding, He starts to confide in them, His secrets. The Lord confides in those who fear him; he makes his covenant known to them. (Psalm 25:14). Prayer and meditation will get you closer to God, and then you will know Him, hear from Him, and see revelation from God.

CHAPTER FIVE

THE SANBALLAT, TOBIAH AND GESHEM IN PRAYER NEHEMIAH 2:4

The enemy's strategies during prayers deeply disturbed Building the wall of protection Nehemiah 3. When Sanballat the Horonite and Tobiah the Ammonite official heard about this, they were very much disturbed that someone had come to promote the welfare of the Israelites. Nehemiah 2:10. God's people live amongst and with their enemies. The same people they want to help are the ones who attack them. Why should Sanballat and Tobiah feel deeply disturbed because a fellow brother is coming to seek the well-being of the people? The answer is the reason why we must pray without ceasing. 1 Thessalonians 5:17. The enemy is constantly looking for every opportunity to attack God's servants. The thieves, killers, and destroyers all have one purpose: to steal, kill, and destroy. Jesus' mission is to give us life and have it abundantly. John 10:10. Its only God who has people's interest at heart and protects them twenty-four seven.

WHO WERE SANBALLAT, TOBIAH, AND GESHEM?

There are enemies in secret, whether you like it or not, as denoted by the Biblical meaning of the name Sanballat is "Bramble-bush, the enemy in secret." Sanballat, Tobiah, and Geshem were three enemies of the Jews who tried to thwart Nehemiah's efforts to restore Jerusalem's walls. "When Sanballat the Horonite and Tobiah the Ammonite official heard about this, they were very much disturbed that someone had come to promote the welfare of the Israelites." Nehemiah 2:10:

But when Sanballat the Horonite, Tobiah the Ammonite official and Geshem the Arab heard about it, they mocked and ridiculed us. "What is this you are doing?" they asked. "Are you rebelling against the king?" Nehemiah 2:19. But when Sanballat the Horonite asked does this mean you're trying to dethrone the monarch?" *Their resentment grew when the construction began: "When Sanballat heard that we were rebuilding the wall, he became angry and was greatly incensed. He ridiculed the Jews,"* Nehemiah 4:1.

God drove out of the Promised Land for the Israelites, the Horonites, and the Ammonites.

Israel's old foes returned decades after the Jewish people initially took possession of the Promised Land, determined to keep Jerusalem in ruins. The Persian king appointed Sanballat, Tobiah, and Geshem as regional governors. Known as a Horonite, Sanballat hails from the Moab city of Horonaim. In a region east of the Jordan River, Tobiah the Ammonite was in charge. Geshem, the Arab, is from the area to the south of Judah, according to the evidence.

Disrupting the Jews' work was a top priority for Sanballat, Tobiah, and Geshem. This trio of assassins intended to harm Nehemiah. Nehemiah 6:2, terrify him with untrue reports vs. 5–6, fool him with false prophets vs. 7–13, and influences Judah's nobles vs.7–19. According to Nehemiah (Nehemiah 13:4), the high priest Eliashib was a descendant of Tobiah, and his grandson married Sanballat's daughter-in-law Nehemiah 13:28. There was no point in battling against God's plan like Sanballat, Tobiah, and Geshem did. Nehemiah 6:15 says the Jews built Jerusalem's wall at a record time. It is possible to learn from the actions of Nehemiah when confronted by his opponents.

It was not Nehemiah who was afraid or worried, but the Lord: "Remember Tobiah and Sanballat, my God, because of what they've done; and remember the prophetess Noadiah as well as how the rest of the prophets tried to scare me" Nehemiah 6:14.

THE STRATEGIES OF THE ENEMY DURING PRAYERS

Strategies are the science or art of combining and employing spiritual warfare to plan and direct large demonic movements and operations against children of God. The three stooges Geshem, Sanballat, and Tobiah repeatedly try to destroy Nehemiah. To harm him four times, they attempt to lure him to a meeting. They aim to provoke him into rebelling against the Persian king. The Holy Spirit wants God's people to be set free from the devil's strongholds and have the Holy Spirit's power on our life strengthened even more. 2 Corinthians 10:4-5 states that "The weapons we fight with are not the weapons of the world. On the contrary, they have divine power to demolish strongholds. [5] We demolish arguments and every pretension that sets itself up against the knowledge of God, and we take captive every thought to make it obedient to Christ."

People should pay close attention to whether they are following the commandments of the Lord Jesus Christ. Those are words of inspiration for believers., In this context, "fighting words" function as a metaphor. All kinds of weapons, castles, lofty things and even captivity come up. These, however, are not weapons of the flesh but the soul. These are not stone fortresses but concepts or arguments that serve as fortifications. We prefer high ideals and the right attitudes rather than high-rise structures. It is not about stealing enemy soldiers but about stealing their ideas. I suppose children of God should think about the symbolic component of the metaphor a little more

What is the definition of a fortified position or stronghold? when it comes to real-world warfare, what is the relevance of fortifications?

A stronghold, in military terms is a defended location Psalm 9:9. "The Lord is a refuge for the oppressed, a stronghold in times of trouble." A tower fortification, a high fortification wall, or a shelter are examples of fortifications or strongholds. As a result, a cliff may act as a defensive stronghold in battle because it is high and inaccessible to the adversary. In 1Samuel 23:14 The Ziph Desert, was a stronghold. "David stayed in the wilderness strongholds and in the hills of the Desert of Ziph. Day after day Saul searched for him, but God did not give David into his hands." Psalm 144:2 makes an allusion to fortress and stronghold.

"He is my loving God and my fortress, my stronghold and my deliverer, my shield, in whom I take refuge, who subdues peoples under me."

Is there a more appropriate location for a "high item" than the summit of a tall cliff or tower? You should go up to the top floor to be safe. If the enemy attacks, it is easier to drive an opponent away from a fortified position than to capture one. He is pulling down Strongholds: Strategies from Ancient and Modern Israel. The situation deeply disturbed them.

Sanballat and Tobiah were in haste to interrupt Nehemiah's vision to build the wall. The enemy does not like the fact that people are going to get married. They hate to see our kids go to school and do well. They do not want to hear things are going well in people's life. Therefore, they will do everything to distract their purpose. Remember, set a goal, keep focused, and ignore detractors and distractors. They will fight against God's people but, they shall not prevail against them. I am with you," says God, "to deliver you." Jeremiah 1:19. People may not be as happy for others. That is normal. However, people should not give up on their aspirations. Use the weapon of prayer day and night to defeat the enemies' plans.

WHEN YOU BECOME A LAUGHINGSTOCK AND ARE DESPISED

I understand the psychology of ridicule; people only want to make fun of others to make (themselves feel and look better). Being a laughingstock is not easy. Even if you understand the real reasons, it doesn't solve the heart of the problem. At this time, the three stooges Geshem, Sanballat, and Tobiah joined forces repeatedly to laugh at Nehemiah. Their purpose was to discourage and make the Jews fear what they could do. People's attitudes can make one feel inferior in society, especially if you are poor or less educated. It can make you feel like someone who has no sense. People usually listen to the rich, intellectuals, and the powerful. You can only discern the difference when you are prayerfully seeking the will of God in life.

Peer pressure can result from needing to fit in, low self-esteem, fear of rejection, and the need to feel secure and safe among peers. The effects of peer pressure can be harmful and have negative consequences. The most common age group for peer pressure is between 12 and 19.

JOSHUA RECEIVES THE COMMISSION FROM GOD

When people pray, the only thing they can do to open their minds is to rise against and beyond any intimidation that might cause them to panic, or feel afraid.

"After the death of Moses the servant of the Lord, the Lord said to Joshua son of Nun, Moses' aide: ² *"Moses my servant is dead. Now then, you and all these people, get ready to cross the Jordan River into the land I am about to give to them— to the Israelites.* ³ *I will give you every place where you set your foot, as I promised Moses.* ⁴ *Your territory will extend from the desert to Lebanon, and from the great river, the Euphrates—all the Hittite country—to the Mediterranean Sea in the west.* ⁵ *No one will be able to stand against you all the days of your life. As I was with Moses, so I will be with you; I will never leave you nor forsake you.* ⁶ *Be strong and courageous, because you will lead these people to inherit the*

land I swore to their ancestors to give them. ⁷ "Be strong and very courageous. Be careful to obey all the law my servant Moses gave you; do not turn from it to the right or to the left, that you may be successful wherever you go. ⁸ Keep this Book of the Law always on your lips; meditate on it day and night, so that you may be careful to do everything written in it. Then you will be prosperous and successful. ⁹ Have I not commanded you? Be strong and courageous. Do not be afraid; do not be discouraged, for the Lord your God will be with you wherever you go." (Joshua 1:1-9)

CHAPTER SIX

RECOGNIZING THE TACTICAL APPROACHES OF THE OPPONENT IN PRAYER

Tobiah, Geshem the Arab, Sanballat, and all my enemies knew that I had rebuilt the wall without a gap. However, I had not put the gates in place until then. Let us meet someplace in the plain of Ono, said Sanballat and Geshem to me. ". Because of their plans to hurt me, I sent them a message saying: "I am working on a huge project, and I will not let you down." What is the point of halting the work if I see you? That is how I responded to the four messages they sent me. When Sanballat sent his aide to me for the fifth time, he had the identical note and a letter in his hands.

NEHEMIAH 6, THE ENEMY'S MOST COMMON METHODS TO OBSTRUCT GOD'S WORK?

Jews had lived in Israel without walls surrounding Jerusalem for centuries. God punished the kings for disobedience by exiling them to Babylon during the days of the kings. After 70 years in exile, Jews began to return to Israel in small groups. When Nehemiah, a man serving under the king of Persia, returned to Jerusalem, God led him to lead the remnant in rebuilding Jerusalem's wall and reviving Israel's religious practices.

Nehemiah had finished the walls but not the gates in Chapter 6. The progress and assurance of completion boosted the enemy's attacks. From the start of the restoration project, opponents tried to halt Nehemiah and the Israelites. Sanballat and other Samaritans urged Israel to retreat. In chapter 2, they raged because someone had come to "advance the Israelites' welfare" (2:10). They taunted them when Israel started building, saying it would fall even if a fox climbed on it (4:10). Their covert action led them to form an army to attack Israel (Nehemiah 4:8). When Nehemiah learned of this, he informed Israel and prepared for an attack. They worked with a brick and a weapon Nehemiah 4:17, and now just the gates remained (6:1).

As a result, Israel's adversaries launch one final big attack, targeting Nehemiah, knowing they can halt the job if they can stop Nehemiah. That is vital for believers to see. This chapter applies primarily to believers, especially leaders in the spiritual battle. Ephesians 6 prepares believers for a similar struggle. Equip yourself with God's armor so that you can stand your ground and do everything when evil comes. Ephesians 6:13. Authors say we always dwell in "the evil day," between Christ's first and second comings when Satan attacks us. The enemy raises attacks to discourage God's people and obstruct his mission. "When the awful day arrives," he remarked. We touched on this in Chapter 4.

In chapter 6, the opponent has a confrontation with Nehemiah. Nehemiah's mission and his life are both in danger due to this. It felt like that Satan was making an aggressive move against Job. He suffers a momentary setback in his health, fortune, and family. When he is under attack, Job needs to keep his composure and not panic.

People can serve the Lord, too, and do the Lord's work, whether a student, teacher, businessperson, or parent. Nehemiah's wall-building was not preaching the gospel but was "accomplished by God" (Nehemiah 6:16). It was a divine work. Likewise, when people execute the Lord's will, wherever He has called them, they are working for him and thus subject to attacks from the enemy.

QUESTION A

1. How do people prepare for attacks, and how to defeat attacks?

Put on the armor of God, which is a godly life, and move forward. However, it would help if you also kept in mind the offensive strategies employed by the enemies.

Satan will use tactics to try and stop good people from developing their spiritual lives since that is his ultimate purpose. He is on the prowl to prevent them from accomplishing the mission that God has entrusted to them. Believers need to be on the lookout for the tricks played by the adversary because he is cunning and will not stop attacking them. In 2 Corinthians 2:11 that this is "in order that Satan might not outwit us. For we are not unaware of his schemes."

Christians become immobilized and ineffective in their

vocations because they are oblivious to the strategies employed by the adversary. As a result of the widespread effects, those in authority, such as Nehemiah, must pay close attention. Satan would use his single bullet to take out the group's leader.

2. How does the devil attack people's lives?

"But while everyone was sleeping, his enemy came and sowed weeds among the wheat, and went away." Matthew 13:25

Satan and his demonic minions will launch their assaults against Christians when they are overtired or sleeping. That enables them to take advantage of a time when the Christians are less able to defend themselves and when their defenses are weaker, which allows them to gain an edge over them.

Nehemiah is aware of the traps that the adversary sets for them during the night, so he devises a plan to work during the night as well.

"I repaired the wall without a gap for Sanballat, Tobiah, Geshem the Arab, and our foes. But I had not installed the gates yet. " When word came to Sanballat, Tobiah, Geshem the Arab and the rest of our enemies that I had rebuilt the wall and not a gap was left in it—though up to that time I had not set the doors in the gates— [2] Sanballat and Geshem sent me this message: "Come, let us meet together in one of the villages[a] on the plain of Ono."

But they were scheming to harm me; [3] so I sent messengers to them with this reply: "I am carrying on a great project and cannot go down. Why should the work stop while I leave it and go down to you?" [4] Four times they sent me the same message, and each time I gave them the same answer.

⁵ Then, the fifth time, Sanballat sent his aide to me with the same message, and in his hand was an unsealed letter 6 in which was written:

"It is reported among the nations—and Geshem says it is true—that you and the Jews are plotting to revolt, and therefore you are building the wall. Moreover, according to these reports you are about to become their king ⁷ and have even appointed prophets to make this proclamation about you in Jerusalem: 'There is a king in Judah!' Now this report will get back to the king; so come, let us meet together."

⁸ I sent him this reply: "Nothing like what you are saying is happening; you are just making it up out of your head."

3. What are joint enemy efforts to stifle God's work?

In this story, the Jews lived in Israel without fortifications around Jerusalem. They rebelled against God throughout the entirety of Babylon's rule, so the city exiled them there as punishment. After 70 years of exile, Nehemiah returned to Israel. He inspired the remnant to rebuild Jerusalem's walls and restore Israel's worship of the living God. Nehemiah had finished the walls but not the gates in Chapter 6. The enemy's schemes to impede the work increased due to the obvious progress and assured completion of the walls. From the start of the restoration project, opponents tried to halt Nehemiah and the Israelites. Sanballat and other Samaritans urged Israel to relent in their planned construction of the wall. In chapter 2, they raged because someone had come to "advance the Israelites' welfare" (2:10). Then when they realized they could not deter Nehemiah and his followers from building the wall, they decided to use ridicule, stating that even "a fox on the wall would cause the wall to crumble". in Chapter 4. (4:10). The opponents and their backers disguised themselves as Jews and covertly formed an army to attack Israel (Nehemiah 4:8). When Nehemiah learned of this, he informed Israel and prepared for an attack. They worked with a brick and a weapon. Nehemiah 4:17, and now just the gates remained (6:1).

As a result, Israel's adversaries launch one final big attack, targeting Nehemiah. If they can stop Nehemiah, they can halt the job. The Jews are the primary target, and the enemy wishes she could end their lives immediately to halt everything they do. That tells us we are always under attack, and must pray without ceasing. This chapter applies primarily to believers and especially leaders in the spiritual battle. Ephesians 6 prepares believers for battle. Put on the full armor of God, so that you can take your stand against the devil's schemes. [12] For our struggle is not against flesh and blood, but against the rulers, against the authorities, against the powers of this dark world and against the spiritual forces of evil in the heavenly realms." Ephesians 6:11-12.

4. The deception strategy employed by the enemy

"When word came to Sanballat, Tobiah, Geshem the Arab and the rest of our enemies that I had rebuilt the wall and not a gap was left in it—though up to that time I had not set the doors in the gates— [2] Sanballat and Geshem sent me this message: "Come, let us meet together in one of the villages on the plain of Ono."

But they were scheming to harm me; [3] so I sent messengers to them with this reply: "I am carrying on a great project and cannot go down. Why should the work stop while I leave it and go down to you?" ⁴ Four times they sent me the same message, and each time I gave them the same answer.". Nehemiah. 6:1-4. The inference is that Judah's foes desired peace and had convened a meeting to achieve it.

The governor of Israel, Nehemiah, decided that making peace was politically wise. Many Jewish lords were pressuring him to make peace at the end of the chapter (v. 16-19). Ignoring the enemy's appeals for a meeting would not be a wise political move. However, according to the text, Nehemiah realized that they had planned to harm him (v. 2), and in response, Nehemiah stated that he was working on a great project and could not abandon it (v. 3)

5. How did Nehemiah defend himself from the enemy's attacks?

First, he achieved it by recognizing the enemy's lies. Recognizing lies is crucial for believers. Consider what Jesus stated about Satan: "You belong to your father, the devil, and you want to carry out your father's desires. He was a murderer from the beginning, not holding to the truth, for there is no truth in him. When he lies, he speaks his native language, for he is a liar and the father of lies." John 8:44. During this time, the Pharisees made another attempt to frame Jesus for a murder they had committed. They were the property of the devil, a liar, and known as the father of lies. People must understand that Satan has been working since the beginning of time to confound believers.

6. There is a history of his ability to deceive many Christians regarding their identity.

    a.   He makes false promises regarding their future.

    b.   He tells them lies about how they should think and dress.

    c.   They are uncertain and have concerns because they have been listening to the devil's falsehoods.

    d.   He makes them feel insecure about their bodies, wealth, cars, and jobs.

    e.   He claims they need this and that to be successful and accepted.

7. The Deception started with how people live.

Agents of Satan lie about what constitutes beauty, what it means to be successful, God, creation, and many other topics.

According to Scripture, the prince of this world is the evil one. John 14:30.

8. Why does the enemy keep lying?

He lies purposefully to keep people from accomplishing God's plan for their lives. Sometimes they even hear these lies from family members or close friends. They may originate from friends, or even their church. They could also arise from the mass media and social media.

Leaders and Christians must grasp this because the enemy will attack them with lies, and they the leaders will continually have to minister to those who have been victims. They have fallen into a spiritual trap because they have accepted the enemy's lies (cf. 2 Tim 2:26). To minister to them, children of God must identify the deception and convey the truth of God's Word. Like Nehemiah, they must be able to spot the devil's trick. How can believers acquire discernment like Nehemiah did so that we don't fall prey to deception by the enemy and can effectively minister to others?

9. Discernment results from having a firm grasp of the Bible.

According to Hebrews 1:19, people who consume milk are analogous to children who have not yet acquired the knowledge necessary to live a righteous life. On the other hand, only adults should be eating solid food because only adults have the maturity and experience required to differentiate between healthy foods and unhealthy foods.

 In Hebrews 5:13-14, The church is compared to spiritual babies because they depend on "milk" instead of "solid food" from the Bible. In the context of Hebrews, there is a tendency to revert to Jewish law. The author of the book of Hebrews believed that the new believers were not mature enough because they could not distinguish between right and wrong in the same way that a child would. Since there was a lack of spiritual development among the group members, they kept falling back into the old covenant practices. Still, the author of Hebrews is trying to make the point that the New Covenant is significantly superior to the old covenant. Christ shines brightest compared to other religious figures, such as Moses, Angels, and the High Priest.

Christians do not reach the highest levels because they do not consistently use the Bible in their lives. People occasionally read or listen to sermons, but because they do not put what they learn into practice, some have no idea how to put what they have learned into action.

As a result, it is simple for the devil to exert his influence over Christians through the various deceptions that he plays on them.

Christians who do not use the Bible consistently in their lives do not have the insight necessary to respond when attacked. Because they have not expanded their knowledge of God's Word, they cannot determine which path would be most beneficial for their professional or personal future. That leaves room for the adversary to behave deceitfully toward other people.

According to Paul, believers should wear a belt of truth, which is a reference to the facts of the Bible. Stand steadfast with the truth belted around your waist in Ephesians 6:14. The belt held the rest of the parts together in ancient armor. As a result, knowing God's Word is an effective defense against the enemy's attacks. Due to the deceitful nature of the enemy's claims, this is true. Is your belt of truth tight? You will be able to tell the devil's falsehoods if you keep using it regularly.

10. Slander and gossip as a weapon of mass destruction

Finally, Sanballat ordered his aide to deliver the same message a fifth time, holding an unopened letter that read: "It is reported among the nations—and Geshem says it is true—that you and the Jews are plotting to revolt, and therefore you are building the wall. Moreover, according to these reports you are about to become their king [7] and have even appointed prophets to make this proclamation about you in Jerusalem: 'There is a king in Judah!' Now this report will get back to the king; so come, let us meet together." I sent him this reply: "Nothing like what you are saying is happening; you are just making it up out of your head." [9] They were all trying to frighten us, thinking, "Their hands will get too weak for the work, and it will not be completed." But I prayed, "Now strengthen my hands." Nehemiah 6:5-9

The adversary attempted to attack Nehemiah using slanderous techniques. On the other side, Sanballat tried to ruin Nehemiah's reputation by coercing him into attending the meeting using threats.

Usually, correspondence with government officials is in the form of a letter that is not open to public inspection. In the beginning, he wrote Nehemiah four personal letters, but after the fourth of those letters, he wrote him an open letter. There is no doubt that this open letter was read in front of Nehemiah and to him. In this account, Sanballat fabricated Nehemiah's ambitions to rule as king (v. 6-7).

Nehemiah's life could have been in jeopardy if Artaxerxes's reputation as a king notorious for swiftly putting down any rebellion had made its way to him.

11. Slanderer, Accuser, and the Devil

A slanderer is synonymous with the accuser, and the devil, and are interchangeable terms. Slander and gossip are standard methods Satan employs to disrupt the work of God's creation, just as some believers do. As a direct consequence, he not only dishonors God but also the people in his immediate environment. He spreads rumors about everybody who will listen to him. It is even within his power to insult believers by accusing them in over ten different ways.

12. What do you think of Satan's lofty depiction in the bible?

Then I heard a loud voice in heaven say: "Now have come the salvation and the power and the kingdom of our God, and the authority of his Messiah.

For the accuser of our brothers and sisters, who accuses them before our God day and night, has been hurled down. (Revelation 12:10).

13. What are some examples of Satan's defamation in the bible?

a. In the sight of God, Satan had brought dishonor upon Job.

b. Satan argues to God in the book of Job that Job follows him only because God has provided him with a prosperous existence and that this is the only reason Job follows God.

c. Satan remarked that Job does not love God, and he suggested that God should physically touch Job's family, wealth, or physique, and see him proved right in his observation.

d. He slandered Job in the presence of God.

e. Satan defamed God in front of Eve. "You will not per-ish, but you will become like God," Satan claimed in the Garden of Eden. Before Eve, Satan slandered God, saying God withheld the best from her and Adam.

f. Through The Pharisees, Satan Slandered Jesus. The Pharisees slandered and accused Christ. They fabricat-ed tens of false witnesses against him to defame him. To put Jesus to death, the chief priests and Sanhedrin hunted for false proof against him. Even though count-less fake witnesses came forward, they could not find any. Finally, two people stood up. Matthew 26:59-60. Satan commonly uses slander. He brings discord and problems to individual Christians and the church by bringing false accusations. That is the devil's character; he is a slanderer.

QUESTION B – APPLICATION
Why does the enemy use slander?

1. The Goal of spreading slander is to undermine the faith of Christians.

"They were all trying to frighten us," Nehemiah remarked, "thinking, their hands will get too weak for the work, and it will not be completed."

(See Nehemiah 6:9). A disheartened and depressed Christian is ineffective in serving God's kingdom. They are frequently so preoccupied with their concerns that they neglect to serve the Lord. As a result, Satan is continually working to weaken and discourage Christians, primarily through slander.

2. Slander is an attempt to divert the Christian's attention to anything else.

When we try to safeguard our reputation, we find ourselves distracted from concentrating on God and the work that He is doing. Satan defames Christians to divert their attention.

3. The purpose of slander is to cause discord.

"A perverse person stirs up conflict, and a gossip separates close friends." Solomon stated. (Prov 16:28). As he sends his whisperers throughout the church, the enemy will use slander to divide the church.

QUESTION C – OBSERVATION

How does Nehemiah respond to the slander? How should people respond to gossip and slander?

1. Confront slander by telling the truth.

Nehemiah 6:8 says, "I sent him this reply: 'Nothing like what you are saying is happening; you are just making it up out of your head.'"

When confronted by the adversary, Nehemiah maintained his composure by speaking the truth. He clarified for them that it was not under the law. There are situations in which the actions that we can take do not allow us to act, and we become immobilized because of our fear. Fear can turn into boldness and self-confidence through prayer.

2. Confront slander by trusting in God.

We see this because Nehemiah prays and puts the situation in God's hands. Nehemiah 6:9 says, "They were all trying to frighten us, believing that "thinking, their hands will get too weak for the work, and it will not be completed.". But I prayed, 'Now strengthen my hands."

When individuals place their confidence in God, there are times when they should keep their mouths shut and not make any excuses for themselves. These are the moments when they should not make any excuses for themselves.

As a result of the untruthfulness of rumors, reality will frequently present itself. After falsely accusing Nehemiah over three occasions, Nehemiah decided not to defend himself. Instead, he chose to maintain his silence and entrust the situation to the care of God. Consider Matthew 26:59-63.

Now the chief priests and the entire Council kept trying to obtain false testimony against Jesus so they might put Him to death. They did not find any, even though false witnesses came forward. But later, two came forward and said, "This man stated, 'I can destroy the temple of God and rebuild it in three days.'" The high priest stood up and said to Him, "Do You offer no answer for what these men are testifying against You?" But Jesus kept silent. And the high priest said to Him, "I place You under oath by the living God, to tell us whether You are the Christ, the Son of God." *What does Matthew chapter 26 mean?*

Children of God need to refute lies with the truth, but there are also times when they need to put their faith in God and allow him to be their defense. (cf. Rom 12:19).

3. Confront slander by living a life that is above reproach.

Those who spread lies about Nehemiah did not appear to have impact. That was because Nehemiah was a man who led a blameless life in every aspect of his being. He was known for his honesty and upright character. As governor of Israel, he brought reform to the corruptness of the previous administration; he never even used his food allotment but instead paid out of his pocket to meet his needs and the needs of others. He was able to bring about reform because of his integrity. (cf. Nehemiah 5:14-18).

There is no indication that either the Jews or Persia's king responded to these rumors. That can only be due to Nehemiah's chaste and holy behavior. If you lead a life that is consistently above reproach, it will be difficult for anyone to spread false information about you because it will be difficult for them to do so

Listen to what Peter commanded of Christians under persecution in Rome: "Live such good lives among the pagans that, though they accuse you of doing wrong, they may see your good deeds and glorify God on the day he visits us. "(1 Peter 2:12). Let this be true of us as well.

QUESTION D – APPLICATION

Why does the enemy try to bring slander into the lives of those who believe in God? Have you ever been the target of malicious rumors or gossip? How did you choose to respond to the situation that arose?

1. The strategy of the enemy is to infiltrate the church with false doctrine.

"One day I went to the house of Shemaiah son of Delaiah, the son of Mehetabel, who was shut in at his home. He said, "Let us meet in the house of God, inside the temple, and let us close the temple doors, because men are coming to kill you—by night they are coming to kill you."

[11] But I said, "Should a man like me run away? Or should someone like me go into the temple to save his life? I will not go!" [12] I realized that God had not sent him, but that he had prophesied against me because Tobiah and Sanballat had hired him. [13] He had been hired to intimidate me so that I would commit a sin by doing this, and then they would give me a bad name to discredit me.

[14] Remember Tobiah and Sanballat, my God, because of what they have done; remember also the prophet Noadiah and how she and the rest of the prophets have been trying to intimidate me. Nehemiah 6:10-14

The enemy then intimidated Nehemiah by giving false teachings. Tobiah and Sanballat hired a prophet named Shemaiah to deceive Nehemiah. He intended to get Nehemiah to protect himself from the enemy by hiding in the temple (v. 10). Shemaiah was trying to give the illusion of a "prophetic utterance.", or give the impression that he was in close communion with God. When we see the prophet "shut in at his home," he was acting out the prophecy. That was common for prophets in the Old Testament. For example, Isaiah prophesied naked against Egypt and Cush to demonstrate how Assyria would conquer them, take them captive, and lead them naked to shame them (Isaiah 20). We also see that Hosea chose to marry a prostitute to represent how Israel was adulterous in her relationship with God (Hosea 1).

Shemaiah said, "Let us meet in the house of God, inside the temple, and let us close the temple doors, because men are coming to kill you—by night they are coming to kill you." (v. 10). This utterance seemed to come in the form of a poetic couplet to trick Nehemiah. However, Nehemiah realized that Sanballat planned to expose him to sin and give him a bad name. Only priests were allowed in the temple, and Nehemiah was not a priest. He would have been disobeying God if he had done what Shemaiah suggested. That is important because one of Satan's common tactics is to lure people away from God and their callings are false teaching and false prophecy. Listen to what Christ said. "Watch out for false prophets. They come to you in sheep's clothing, but inwardly they are ferocious wolves. [16] By their fruit you will recognize them. Do people pick grapes from thornbushes, or figs from thistles? Matthew 7:15-16

Jesus warned his followers to be on the lookout for false prophets. *Anti-Christ Politics vs. the Politics of Jesus | Sojourners.* They come to us dressed as shepherds but are wolves in sheep's clothing. The people will be able to identify them based on the fruits they bear. However, they are vicious wolves bent on wreaking havoc. The adversary has successfully led people astray through his many false teachers. Paul said this. "For such people are false apostles, deceitful workers, masquerading as apostles of Christ. [14] And no wonder, for Satan himself masquerades as an angel of light. [15] It is not surprising, then, if his servants also masquerade as servants of righteousness. Their end will be what their actions deserve.". 2 Corinthians 11:13-15.

The fact that his servants may masquerade as servants of righteousness is not surprising. Paul said these people were masquerading as servants of right in the church. That is still happening today, and we must be aware of it. Consider what Paul taught Timothy about the last days:

"The Spirit clearly says that in later times some will abandon the faith and follow deceiving spirits and things taught by demons. [2] Such teachings come through hypocritical liars, whose consciences have been seared as with a hot iron. 1 Timothy 4:1-2. Paul said false teachers and instructions would explode in the last few days. A new cult of Christianity pops up every day, and people from the church follow them. If this continues to increase these last days, how much of the knowledge that Christians need to survive these times, would be available?

QUESTION F - INTERPRETATION # 1
How did Nehemiah know this was a false prophecy?
How can believers know?

1. Nehemiah analyzed their message by contrasting it with the Bible

Nehemiah knew this was a false prophesy because he knew it would be impossible for him to enter the temple and close the doors. The fact that the prophet talked about completing the entry indicates that he was calling him to join the Holy Place, which was only for priests (Num 18:7).2 For him to enter could even have led to his death. A king in the Old Testament entered the Holy place to offer a sacrifice, and God struck him with leprosy (cf. 2 Chr 26:19). He, no doubt, evaluated this prophecy by knowing Scripture. God would never tell him to enter a forbidden area of the temple.

The best protection from false teachers and false doctrine is through diligent study of the Word of God. Listen to the story of the Bereans. Now the Bereans were of more noble character than the Thessalonians, for they received the message with great eagerness and examined the Scriptures every day to see if what Paul said was true. Acts 17:1. God is looking for Christians who will study the Bible and challenge the teachings of their leaders. A summons from God to all who have put their confidence in him is to be a "noble" Christian and exercise extreme prudence, especially regarding prophecies from men of God in the 21st century. That is especially important concerning predictions made by men of God in the last days

2. Nehemiah was aware of his own identity.

In addition to his role as Israel's governor, Nehemiah served God and the Israelites as a priest and prophet. Because he was doing both the wills of God and man, he could not sin against either of them. Nehemiah said, "Should a man like me hide?" God's people are vulnerable to falling for Satan's lies because we do not understand who we are in Christ. Scripture portrays this reality in the New Testament as being actual for us. If you are unaware of who you are in Christ, you may try to find your identity in things such as your possessions, your level of education, the people in your life, or even sin. They will search everywhere for answers if they do not know who they are.

Christ, for instance, instructed his disciples about their identity as children of God so that they would not have to struggle with fear and worry about the future provisions of the church. Pay attention to what he says: "So do not worry, saying, 'What shall we eat?' or 'What shall we drink?' or 'What shall we wear?' 32 For the pagans run after all these things, and your heavenly Father knows that you need them. 33 But seek first his kingdom and his righteousness, and all these things will be given to you as well.". Matthew 6:31–33

Jesus said "Look at the birds of the air; they do not sow or reap or store away in barns, and yet your heavenly Father feeds them. Are you not much more valuable than they? 27 Can any one of you by worrying add a single hour to your life?" Matthew 6:26-27. Finding the underlying cause of who you are will set us free from our adversary's deception. The importance of knowing God's Word cannot be stressed enough when defending ourselves against the various false teachings that are becoming more prevalent as the end times draw near. Nehemiah knew that going into the holy area of the temple would be sinning. It belongs solely to the priests. Nehemiah, on the other hand, was aware of his roles as a leader in Israel and a servant of God. By being aware of who we are, we can avoid falling prey to Satan's schemes.

QUESTION G - APPLICATION # 2

*In what ways has knowing your identity in Christ helped
set you free from various sins and temptations?*

1. It Is The enemy's psychological warfare tactic.

"I realized that God had not sent him, but that he had prophesied against me because Tobiah and Sanballat had hired him. [13] He had been hired to intimidate me so that I would commit a sin by doing this, and then they would give me a bad name to discredit me.

[14] Remember Tobiah and Sanballat, my God, because of what they have done; remember also the prophet Noadiah and how she and the rest of the prophets have been trying to intimidate me." "Moreover, they kept reporting to me his good deeds and then telling him what I said. And Tobiah sent letters to intimidate me." Nehemiah 6:12-14 and 19

Although we talked about this topic a little bit earlier, it merits its own separate discussion because it appears twice in this section. We read about it in Nehemiah chapter 6, verses 13-14, and then again in verse 19. Instilling fear and anxiety in people spread deceptive teachings and correspondence from the adversary. Nehemiah's adversaries effectively used fear as one of the primary weapons in their arsenal. Tobiah and Sanballat's plan to intimidate Nehemiah was to bring a false prophet, which they hoped would lead to the prophet's conversion to sin. Tobiah also sent him threatening letters (v. 19). People were also afraid of having derogatory terms directed at them. They all said, "their hands will get too weak for the work, and it will not be completed." to discourage us.

Through slander, deception, and the letters Nehemiah received, the adversary attempted to instill a sense of terror in him. And this is what the Devil does to people under his influence. People who claim to have faith in God are constantly the target of his efforts to instill in them a sense of dread and dreadfulness. When Peter hears Satan roaring, he compares him to a ravenous lion. According to what it says in 1 Peter 5:8, "Be alert and of sober mind. Your enemy the devil prowls around like a roaring lion looking for someone to devour."

Why does a lion roar, and what does it hope to accomplish with it? He employs a cunning strategy to terrify his prey into giving in to him so that he can pounce on it and consume it. Fear was the primary means by which the devil opposed God's work. Similarly, Satan frequently used terror to subjugate those who believed. The devil also takes advantage of our anxieties. Nehemiah became hostage by Tobiah and Sanballat, who played on his fears. They planned to spread rumors about him in the hopes of frightening him and infuriating the king. To coerce him into attacking, his adversary threatened to kill him.

QUESTION H - INTERPRETATION # 2
Why does Satan specifically use fear as a tactic to get believers and leaders to do what he wants them to do?

To begin, Satan uses fear to discourage believers from conducting the will of God. That is something mentioned in the parable of the talents. Matthew 25:24-25 says, " "Then the man who had received one bag of gold came. 'Master,' he said, 'I knew that you are a hard man, harvesting where you have not sown and gathering where you have not scattered seed. [25] So I was afraid and went out and hid your gold in the ground. See, here is what belongs to you.'

It is common to hear of believers who have only one talent but do not use it because they are afraid of what others will think of them. They cannot pray, spread the gospel, or serve in leadership positions. That renders them unable to serve the Lord because it paralyzes them. Even among those who claim to serve God, the enemy engages in psychological warfare. Additionally, Christians struggle with anxiety, which hinders their performance. Anxiety was something that both Moses and Gideon felt while they were doing it. Believers will have a challenging time if they worry about Satan attacking them.

According to Matthew 13:22, "That Sower whose seed fell among thorns," when people hear the message that God has for them, the worldly cares and the deception of wealth choke them and hinder them from producing fruit. Jesus' Parable of the Sower (Matthew 13:3-23).

Most people are chronic worriers. Because of the pressures of this life, the Word could not produce any fruit when planted in the thorny ground (fear). The thorn in the side that worry creates for Christians makes it difficult for them to hear the Word of God. Even if people listen to the Word of God and acknowledge that they agree with it, their fears prevent it from affecting their lives. As a direct consequence, God cannot accomplish His work within them. It suffocates the power which resides in the Word of God.

Fear plays a role in all three of Satan's strategies for leading believers astray.

The adversary had a strategy in mind for dealing with Nehemiah when it came to him. He was trying to instill fear in Nehemiah in the hopes that he would run into the temple and commit an act of idolatry, thereby undermining not only his authority but also the confidence of the people in him. Fear and insecurity are typically the root causes of a person's sinful behavior. Abraham lied to Pharaoh about his wife's beauty because he feared the king would take his life if he did not protect her. Abraham sinned against God when he wed a second woman, Hagar, because he was anxious that he would not be able to father a child with his first wife, Sarah. The sin he committed due to his fear is representative of the sins committed by the rest of us. Our typical activities are the same. Fear is one of Satan's most effective tools for luring believers into a state of depression. In Nehemiah, chapter six, verse nine says about the workers, "They tried to scare us by declaring that their hands would become too weak for the work and that they would not be able to finish it."

Nehemiah suffers weakness in chapter 4 at the hands of Tobiah and Sanballat, which prevents him from completing the project. According to Christian who is depressed contributes less to the advancement of God's kingdom. Depression is a direct result of anxiety. Satan plants seeds of fear to undermine and demoralize those who believe.

QUESTION I - APPLICATION # 3

How do we combat the tactic of fear?

1. A child of God needs to understand that fear is not from God to realize that it is possible to overcome it.

The apostle Paul said to Timothy: Because God did not give people a spirit of cowardice but a spirit of power, love, and self-discipline. (2 Timothy 1:7). As Paul tells Timothy, God has not given His people a spirit of fear. He calls Timothy to recognize that his insecurities, in ministry, were not from God. Paul said to the Philippians, "Be anxious for nothing" (4:6). We should not accept fear from God. Indeed, there are healthy fears, such as the fear of the Lord, but fear that keeps us from serving God or trusting him is not from the Lord. Paul commands us to let the peace of Christ rule in our hearts (Col 3:15).

2. To conquer our fears, we need to acknowledge that God is our source of strength.

Paul did not simply tell Timothy to reject fear; he also gave him reasons. Look again at what he said: Because God did not give us a spirit of cowardice but a spirit of power, love, and self-discipline, people can say that "for this reason" (2 Timothy 1:7). Timothy, there is no need to be afraid. Look at God's resources. He has given us these resources: power, love, and discipline. God has given us the same resources as Timothy: passion, love, and discipline.

3. A prayer is a powerful tool that can overcome anxiety and other negative emotions.

Nehemiah immediately responded when they told not once but twice, in both the open letter and the vision from the false prophet, that he had good reason to be afraid.

He prayed throughout the process as the enemy tried to intimidate the Jews, saying, "Their hands will get weak, and they will not finish." But I prayed, "Now strengthen my hands." Nehemiah 6:9. Remember Tobiah and Sanballat, O my God, because of what they have done; remember the prophet Noadiah and all the prophets who have tried to intimidate me. Nehemiah 6:14. Encouraging people to battle fear similarly in the New Testament. Remember what Paul told the Philippians:

"Do not be anxious about anything, but in every situation, by prayer and petition, with thanksgiving, present your requests to God. [7] And the peace of God, which transcends all understanding, will guard your hearts and your minds in Christ Jesus." Philippians 4:6-7.

Combating the spirit of Noadiah, the prophetess, can be done by

a. choosing not to fear,

b. choosing to pray about everything, and

c. giving thanks for everything.

People find themselves hindered from doing the work God has called them to do, because there is no peace in their marriages, they are constrained financially and continue struggling with life's difficulties. They have consciously decided to be anxious and are intent on being afraid. They have agreed to refrain from praying about everything. And finally, most Christians do not express gratitude for everything they have. There is whining, and there is agitation, which escalate the conflict; as a result, the adversary continues to gain the upper hand.

Those who practice each of these disciplines will be the only ones to receive the promise of peace. Nehemiah overcame his anxiety by turning to prayer, and everyone else must do the same. Do people understand that everyone, including Nehemiah, has at least one adversary? There are certain occurrences in people's lives and the lives of their families that the adversary intends to use to paralyze them with fear; Satan desires to render families helpless by burdening them with worries. Nevertheless, God wants his people to have peace so that they can continue to serve him. This is the strategy that the adversary employs to fight against the people of God.

J. APPLICATIONS QUESTION:

What are common fears that the enemy uses against people? How do these fears immobilize or affect them? How is God calling believers to be free from these fears to serve him better?

1. The adversary's strategy is to launch an attack as soon as they have been victorious.

"So the wall was completed on the twenty-fifth of Elul, in fifty-two days.

16 When all our enemies heard about this, all the surrounding nations were afraid and lost their self-confidence, because they

realized that this work had been done with the help of our God. [17] Also, in those days the nobles of Judah were sending many letters to Tobiah, and replies from Tobiah kept coming to them. [18] For many in Judah were under oath to him, since he was son-in-law to Shekaniah son of Arah, and his son Jehohanan had married the daughter of Meshullam son of Berekiah. [19] Moreover, they kept reporting to me his good deeds and then telling him what I said. And Tobiah sent letters to intimidate me". Nehemiah 6:15-19

It says in verse 15 that the wall took 52 days to build, and all the surrounding nations feared it because they realized God had helped. You might expect an end to the memoirs of Nehemiah or if "They lived happily ever after" because the wall finishes, but that does not happen. The enemy attacked again immediately. The next attack came through the nobles of Judah, who would have been very influential, as Judah was the royal line. They were bound to Tobiah through marriage, and the people shared everything Nehemiah said with him. (ref) *7. Recognizing the Tactics of the Enemy | Bible. org.* At the same time, they continually spoke good words about Tobiah. However, these good words were ingenious, as Tobiah kept sending intimidating letters to Nehemiah (v. 19).

The fact that they are attacking so soon after a victory is a strategy that Satan frequently employs. In Luke 4:13, immediately following Satan's temptation of Jesus, we receive a glimpse into Satan's opportunistic nature. When he had finished tempting him, the Devil left him until an appropriate time (Luke 4:13). Satan is always looking for the perfect opportunity to launch his attack on the world. Despite Jesus' victory, Satan continued to search for a way in and stood ready to launch an assault. After achieving success, Jesus and Peter appear to have engaged in antagonistic behavior in Matthew 16:15–23. Jesus questioned his disciples by asking,

"But what about you?" he asked. "Who do you say I am?"[16] Simon Peter answered, "You are the Messiah, the Son of the living God." (Who do men think that they see in me?) Peter referred to Jesus as "the Christ, the Son of God" throughout the gospels. Christ greeted him with blessings and then told him, Jesus replied, "Blessed are you, Simon son of Jonah, for this was not revealed to you by flesh and blood, but by my Father in heaven. [18] And I tell you that you are Peter, and on this rock I will build my church, and the gates of Hades will not overcome it. [19] I will give you the keys of the kingdom of heaven; whatever you bind on earth will be bound in heaven, and whatever you loose on earth will be loosed in heaven.")

God blessed Peter, which turned out to be a significant victory. After receiving Christ's blessing, Peter experienced a sense of superiority. However, within minutes later, Jesus would make a substantial stumble. Christ revealed to his disciples that he would suffer death on a cross and then rise from the dead after three days. Peter immediately corrected Jesus, who asserted that he would not perish. Christ responded, "Get behind me, Satan, for it is offensive to me that you are here." After Peter's victory, his adversary discovered a way to communicate with others by using him as a conduit.

In the same vein, the battle between Elijah and the priests of Baal described in the 18th chapter of 1 King ended with Elijah victorious. God had sent fire down from the heavens to consume the altar, and Elijah had all the priests killed. However, in the

19th chapter of 1 King, Queen Jezebel made a threatening statement to Elijah, prompting him to flee for his life. After suffering his most significant loss from what was previously his greatest victory, he fell into a deep depression and even prayed to God to take his own life. Satan is perpetually on the lookout for a fortuitous time, which in most cases occurs not long after a victory. Christians climb to the mountain's peak, only to find themselves falling back into the valley. That is a strategy that the adversary employs frequently.

Students would go on a retreat during the school year and then return to school with a rekindled zeal for God. However, not long after they returned home, they experienced a significant decline in their spiritual state.

After having an experience on the summit of the mountain, they almost immediately had another one down in the valley. People can become lost on the internet, struggle with depression, or get into an intense argument with a close friend or member of their family. These are just the potential outcomes. There was nothing peculiar about it. The moment immediately following one of Satan's defeats is his preferred opportunity to launch an attack

People are vulnerable to temptation when they forget their devotional time and go to work. That frequently happens because our natural inclination is to relax after a victory, and lower our guard. After attending a service filled with the Holy Spirit, couples people find it difficult to avoid getting into an argument.

"Let us be as vigilant after the victory as we were before the battle," the commander commanded. Since we are familiar with the tactics employed by our opponent, we have a responsibility to keep the same level of vigilance both before and after we have achieved victory.

K. APPLICATION QUESTION:

How has the enemy's tactic of immediately launching an attack right after a victory or a spiritual high played out in your life? What can humans do to better safeguard themselves against falling prey to this tactic?

1. The strategy of the opponent is to infiltrate our positions by compromising ourselves.

One of the enemy's last strategies against Nehemiah was infiltration through compromise. As mentioned, the nobles of Judah were under oath to Tobiah through marriage. Like other Samaritans, Tobiah was ethnically mixed. He was part Jewish and part Ammonite (cf. Nehemiah 2:9). His name in Hebrew meant "God is good." He had married a daughter of Judah, and the tribe of Judah had a considerable influence throughout Israel. (ref) *7. Recognizing the Tactics of the Enemy | Bible.org.*

Proverbs 28:4 says that people who abandon the law praise the wicked, but those who keep the law resist those people. The nobles were trying to reach a compromise. They made a mistake by marrying off their daughter to an outsider, which they should not have done, and they also showed their support for Tobiah, who had been an enemy of Israel in the past. Their actions are clear to see because of both mistakes.

That takes place within the church, most notably among the younger members. It is common to find them promoting specific musicians who spread messages opposed to God. They will be watching shows that either teach other immoral ways to live or dishonor God's design for the roles of people in the world. (ref) *God's Design for Man and Woman Book Review - CBMW*. However, in addition to showing concern and listening attentively, they also offer praise. They brag about it constantly. They give their respect and honor to those who dishonor God. Those who reject the law provide credit to those who break it.

The nobles reported Taibah's successful work and Nehemiah's words throughout the book. A compromise was the most dangerous of Nehemiah's attacks, even though the two disagreed on a solution. Nehemiah reveals much later that this compromise was still practice of over ten years after the wall's completion, even after the reforms described in chapters 8-12. By the time we reach Nehemiah 13:7, Tobiah has already taken up residence in the temple. Israel had broken the rules by allowing a person who was not a priest to use one of the rooms in the temple.

In chapter 13, the Israelites resumed their practice of marrying foreign women despite God's prohibition against doing so. It was the same compromise Solomon made, leading to Israel turning their backs on God and bringing judgment upon them. Settlement is one of the most dangerous strategies employed by the adversary; it frequently destroys individual Christians, churches, and other Christian organizations. It is comparable to a weed that is difficult to remove. It can remain rooted for years when it wreaks havoc on an otherwise healthy harvest.

QUESTION L - INTERPRETATION

Why does the enemy put in so much effort to convince believers to compromise their values and give in to temptation?

1. As quickly as yeast can multiply...

...so can compromise relationships. Says Paul, "Your boasting is not good. Don't you know that a little yeast leavens the whole batch of dough?1 Cor 5:6. Ministries or congregations can become compromised very quickly. It will make it possible for more evil and significant strongholds to exist in one's life and the community. As Paul predicted, it is getting worse.

2. When People compromise, ...

...they forfeit God's blessing. In the words of King David, "Blessed is the one who does not walk in step with the wicked or stand in the way that sinners take or sit in the company of mockers," " (Psalm 1:1). As David stated, those who compromise with God's plan for their lives forfeit the blessing. The only person who receives blessing is the one who does not follow the advice of the wicked. What is the evil's plan? Is any statement or action express the antithesis of what God has revealed to us? Books, movies, music, and podcasts fall under this category. According to James, being friends with the world means being at odds with God (4:4). Compromise is the cause of Christians' spiritual blindness.

3. Compromise damages our intimacy with God.

Regarding being YOKED with unbelievers, consider what Paul said. "Do not be yoked together with unbelievers. For what do righteousness and wickedness have in common? Or what fellowship can light have with darkness?"

"Come out from them and be separate, says the Lord. Touch no unclean thing, and I will receive you."[18] And, "I will be a Father to you, and you will be my sons and daughters, says the Lord Almighty." (2 Cor. 6:14, 17-18.). The perils of marrying an unbeliever are evident in these Scriptures, but their consequences are profound. Whoever chooses to leave the world, Paul says, "I will be your father, you will be my sons and daughters" (v.18). Given that he is writing to Christians, which seems like an odd premise. Paul is writing to the church in Corinth. What does he mean when he says, "I'll be your father"? Intimacy with God is a promise of this passage. Because of compromise, Christians miss the closeness God desires. God, where are you? I cannot hear your voice!?" they yell.

They do not enjoy their time in the Word or church. They may not be able to hear the voice of the Father or fully feel his love because of the shame.

Paul tells us that to receive God's promise; we must separate ourselves from the rest of the world. Compromise is a powerful force that spreads rapidly. Christians have died because of compromise. "The enemy continues to attack," Nehemiah says at the close of the chapter. What are people compromising on? Even a little leaven can transform an entire batch (1 Cor 5:6). Satan requires a small area to damage a harvest to render a Christian or a Christian community ineffective. Sin will continue to spread.

QUESTION M – APPLICATION # 6

How have you observed Christians and Christian societies suffering from compromise? Are you confronted by your rival with endless opportunities to make a deal?

Summary

A crucial part of the responsibilities of a godly leader is to be aware of the strategies that our adversaries use to compromise not only our security but also the security of our communities.

How exactly does Satan intend to thwart God's plans for the world? The devil's go-to weapons are slander and gossip, and he will use them against God, us, and other people. The adversary's deception manifests in this manner: Lying is in his blood, and he is the progenitor of those who lie. In the conflict for the faithful's eternal souls, the adversary's strategy is to employ repetition.

The adversary's strategy for psychological warfare is to instill fear and discouragement in their targets. One of the ways that the adversary penetrates our minds is through the dissemination of false teaching. To protect ourselves from falling for deception, we need to have a solid understanding of both the Bible and who we are. The strategy of our opponent to launch an attack right after one of our victories requires us to remain vigilant. That is possible that the most dangerous course of action for an infiltrator to take is to compromise their position. The damage to one's relationship with God because of this is beyond repair.

CHAPTER SEVEN

THE POWER AND BENEFITS THAT COMES FROM PRAYING LATE AT NIGHT

The hearts of the people
cry out to the Lord.
You walls of Daughter Zion,
let your tears flow like a river
day and night;
give yourself no relief,
your eyes no rest.
[19] Arise, cry out in the night,
as the watches of the night begin;
pour out your heart like water
in the presence of the Lord.
Lift up your hands to him
for the lives of your children,
who faint from hunger
at every street corner.

THE POWER AND BENEFITS THAT COMES FROM PRAYING LATE AT NIGHT

Throughout the night, saints occasionally raise their hands in prayer and lament at the beginning of each watch. When they pray and raise their hands toward your holy places, they offer supplications to you. (Psalm 28:2). A blessing at dawn profoundly affects people's lives, and any damage control mechanisms employed by the adversary against God's people become useless. As dawn draws near, the adversary starts preparing for all the malicious activities that demons conduct during the day. There is a window of opportunity for people to stop any evil plot attempting to hurt the children of God, and we ought to make use of this window of opportunity.

The people of God ought to prioritize cultivating dynamic prayer habits that they can practice at any time of the day or night. Everything, including prayer is possible when the time is right. The saints can accomplish their tasks only successfully with the blessings of the saints offered at midnight, just as Satan and his minions accomplish their tasks while most people are asleep.

THE MESSAGE BEHIND THE PARABLE OF THE WEEDS

However, while everyone was sleeping, his adversary arrived, sowed weeds among the wheat, and snuck away. The weeds appeared simultaneously when the wheat began to sprout and bear grain. The proprietor's employees approached him and asked, " "The owner's servants came to him and said, 'Sir, didn't you sow good seed in your field? Where then did the weeds come from?'' ? (The verses in Matthew 13:25-27)

The dynamic and personal quality of our devotion to God improves when we become more like God in his compassion for others and learn to share in that compassion ourselves. An important illustration of this is in the book of Lamentations, where Jeremiah expresses his sorrow and tears through worship and intercession. He worries about the wickedness and punishment that will befall the people of God. Similarly, God requires people to intercede on behalf of their families and nations in prayer, asking for God's grace, salvation, and restoration to receive upon them and their communities. That is an atonement for the sins committed by those closest to them.

When people meditate or pray, they should not try to suppress their feelings; instead, they should express themselves let their feelings and emotions loose. In our prayers, we should make supplications for forgiveness, repentance, and a change of heart on the part of those who have harmed us. In addition, we should make supplications to end inflation and corruption in public sectors. These are all things for which we should be praying to God. It is important to remember that God wants to hear from you, so do not be afraid to communicate with him about anything that is going on in your mind.

ACT AS IF YOU WERE THE NIGHT WATCHMAN.

The Bible provides references to guards responsible for keeping an eye out for potential threats to their physical well-being. Consider the following paragraph as an illustration. "Joram saw the company of Jehu as they came and said, "I see a company." Joram then ordered, "Take an equestrian, send him to meet them, and let him say, "Is it peace?" (2 Kings 9:17, ESV). The Watchmen and the Company had the responsibility and the duty of ensuring the safety of agricultural lands and vineyards during the harvest season (Isaiah 5:1–2; Matthew 21:33; Mark 12:1). In addition, they performed the role of sentinels, who heralded the start of each new day (Psalm 130:6; Isaiah 21:11–12).

There is a spiritual interpretation of "watchmen" in the Bible. The Prophets bore the responsibility of serving as spiritual security guards over the souls of God's people. God told a prophet: "You are Israel's watchman. Attention! Warn them! " (Ezekiel 33:7; Hosea 9:8). As security guards, the prophets encouraged God's people to live pure lives and warned them of the dangers of disobeying the Lord and engaging in evil. As security guards, the prophets were responsible for warning evil people about the judgment and destruction that would occur if they continued to behave in such a way.

The spiritual watchers over Israel bore a significant burden of obligation before the Lord. If a prophet failed to fulfill the responsibilities God had given him, he jeopardized his own life. Then you need to send a warning to your people, which should go something like this: "When I bring my sword against a land, and the people choose one among themselves and make him their watchman, and if they hear the sword approaching and sound the trumpet, then anyone who hears the trumpet but disregards it because they have not heeded the warning, then there will be a disaster for everyone that hears it." They should have heeded the warning sounded by the trumpet, but instead, they chose to ignore it, and as a result, they perished along with everyone else.

They had only needed to pay attention to the warning, and they would have been able to stay out of trouble and rescue themselves.

However, if the watchman sees the sword approaching and does not sound the trumpet to alert the people, and then the sword comes and kills someone, then the person who received the death will die due to their sin, but the watchman will be responsible." (Ezekiel 33:2–6).

If a guard neglected or disobeyed the Lord's Word, he left his people vulnerable to danger and suffering (Isaiah 56:10). A devoted guard has only one option: advise them to repent, regardless of whether he survives.

He must obey the mandate to fulfill his duty (Ezekiel 33:9). The concept of spiritual guards serving as church leaders survives in the New Testament, which instructs followers to "Listen to your spiritual leaders and obey the advice that they give." They have as their responsibility the monitoring of your spiritual health, and they are accountable to God for their work. Leaders should find a way to give them a reason to embrace this challenge with joy rather than grief. That would certainly not work to their benefit (Hebrews 13:17, NLT).

In a different sense, God calls not just the leaders of the Christian community but all Christians to be guards. Jesus cautioned His disciples to "watch and pray" so they would not succumb to temptation. The Spirit is willing, but the body is weak (Mark 14:38). Our Lord will return one day, so let us prepare for his arrival by keeping our lamps burning, like servants awaiting their master's return after a wedding dinner. When he knocks, they can open the door to him immediately. When their master arrives, it will benefit those servants if their master finds them watching. (Matthew 25:1-13)

In all seriousness, remember that he will require to be served, invite him to sit down, and then tend to his requirements. It will be advantageous for those servants whose master finds them ready whenever he comes, no matter when he arrives; whether in the middle of the night or close to the start of the day. People ought to be vigilant, for if the property owner had been aware of the time the burglar was going to arrive, he would not have permitted the front door to be broken down and pushed open. Everyone, too, needs to be prepared since the Son of Man will come at an hour when they are not anticipating his arrival (Luke 12:35–40). (Luke 12:35–40).

During the night prayer, people should be willing to pray and intercede on behalf of those who serve God. Raise voices in worship and pray to God to save the wayward children of the 21st century and those who suffer under the oppression of poor governance and wicked men. God appointed the watchman to warn His people of their sins in the book of Ezekiel. "Son of man, speak to your people and say to them: 'When I bring the sword against a land, and the people of the land choose one of their men and make him their watchman, [3] and he sees the sword coming against the land and blows the trumpet to warn the people, [4] then if anyone hears the trumpet but does not heed the warning and the sword comes and takes their life, their blood will be on their own head. (Ezekiel 33:2). Each of us is assigned the role of a watchman, whose duty it is to keep an eye out for any theft occurring inside our respective jurisdictions. If we do not pray, God will hold us responsible for all the failures in our own lives and those of our churches, families, children, and our nation.

In conclusion, Isaiah 62:6-7 exhorts the people of God to pray earnestly, not to let God rest but to rouse him with unrelenting pleas, for God to maintain the promises until the very end.

CHAPTER EIGHT

THE DELIBERATION DURING
THE PRAYERS

*"But whose delight is in the law of the Lord, and who
meditates on his law day and night. (Psalm 1:2)*

The Hebrew word Hagah refers to something not synonymous
with the English word "meditation," which may serve as
a guide for mental practice; *deliberation* is a synonym for the
Hebrew word. In Hebrew thought, meditating on the Scriptures
involves either repeating them in a low, monotonous tone or
engaging in prolonged and careful consideration of them while
completely shutting out any distractions from the outside world
It is essential to remember that meditation does not take the
form of speech or the transmission of a sincere request; instead,
it can take the form of cud-chewing animals and how they eat
their food.

What are the benefits of chewing the cud, and why is doing so beneficial in the first place? *How Do Cows Eat Their Food | Find Out Here | All Animals Faq.*

Various animals, such as cattle, deer, sheep, goats, and antelope, are known to chew their cud. When animals that chew cud consume their food, a portion of it remains in a pouch specifically designed for that purpose within the animal's stomach. After it has finished regurgitating the food it had previously stored, it will then begin to chew the stored food, which is called the cud..

The term "chewing the cud" refers to a motion that assists digestion (the process of breaking down substances) and the absorption of nutrients. Animals that chew the cud can evade the responsibility of chewing their food when eating because they reserve some of their meal to chew again later. That allows these animals to avoid the obligation of chewing their food. Because of this, even when they are in a defensive position with their heads down, they can still consume a considerable quantity of grass in a brief period.

According to Joshua 1:8–9, the patriarchs needed to concentrate on the word continuously during the day and at night. Therefore, prayer and meditation are examples of spiritual "cud-chewing," which refers to a process in which the spirit, soul, and body modify the training received at that moment of meditation. Prayer and meditation are also examples of spiritual "cud-chewing."

This Book of the Law is not to leave the mouth of your mouth at any time, and you are to meditate on it day and night so that you may observe and conduct everything that is stated in it precisely as it indicates. You will have a smooth trip and be successful when you get to your destination. Have I not been evident in my directions to you? Be bold and courageous; do not be frightened, and do not become dismayed, for the Lord your God is with you wherever you go.

1.   *Church of the Nations - Sun Stand Still: Prayer & Audacious Faith - COTN.*

2.   *"'Have I Not Commanded You? Be Strong and of Good Courage; Do Not Be Afraid, nor Be Dismayed, for the Lord Your God Is with You Wherever You Go.'" Florida Times Union, Florida Times Union, 19 Sept. 2018, p. 1.* Be courageous.

"May these words of my mouth and this meditation of my heart be pleasing in your sight, Lord, my Rock and my Redeemer. - Psalm 19:14

A person's reaction towards hardship clearly indicates the state of their heart, or true character. People's actions and words are intimately related to what they think internally. Additionally, the two work together. People should examine their hearts more frequently and thoroughly. When everything goes as planned, peoples' true natures remain unseen. However, when situations are complicated, that is when people discover what is secretly residing in those areas of their hearts that influence what they say or how they behave; traits that have always existed, but lay dormant, then surface.

When people find themselves in precarious circumstances, they have two distinct courses of action from which to choose. (1) Remain placid with the conviction that they can prevail and have faith in God's provision for them. (2) Anxiety, which causes people to have second thoughts, which leads to their acting or speaking in a manner that is not beneficial. They would have reached a point where they could no longer ignore that there was always more going on beneath the surface. The expressions "when the rubber hits the road" and "you find out what you're capable of" become more accurate. In those moments, people will need to make the deliberate decision to deal with what has been made evident to them; if they do not, they run the risk of being deceived, which can impede the development of their experience with God and their connection to him. People who have faith in God allow the convictions they feel deep within themselves to dictate how they live their lives and their pronouncements. *What Each Zodiac Sign Is Unapologetically Picky About - YourTango.*

Possess an understanding of the power of your words

Proverbs advises listeners to consider their words carefully and to speak only when necessary. James 1:19. Words can both give life and take it away. If you have a passion for conversation, you will enjoy the results of your remarks. Mark Twain infamously said, "Better to Remain Silent and Be Thought a Fool than to Speak and Remove All Doubt". *"All Doubt – Quote Investigator.* Realizing that you do not need always to say something can help you recognize the value of speaking less frequently.

Proverbs 19:14. It is possible that people will be able to talk for a while, but sooner or later, the truth will become apparent and reveal what's going on. People can sway others' perceptions of themselves and their lives through the words they say because they use those words daily to communicate with one another and share information. To put it another way, the wise man Solomon said, "Speakers have the power of life and death, and those who love their tongue will reap the fruits of it."

"May these words of my mouth and this meditation of my heart be pleasing in your sight, Lord, my Rock and my Redeemer." Psalms 19:14

These passages from the Bible ought to serve as a roadmap for everyone as they conduct a thoughtful examination of themselves to determine whether the things they say and the goals they pursue are congruent with one another. If this is not the case, then they are lying to themselves, their neighbors, and, most importantly, to God. According to John 10:10, Jesus told those who followed him, "I have come to give your life, and I have come to give your life to the full." Therefore, everyone needs to put that promise into practice so that the light of God can continue to shine through their words and the people around them can find life and hope through the language they use.

The seven stages that make up an effective meditation routine

1. Write:

Take it into consideration, ensure it is ingrained in your memory, and remind yourself frequently throughout the day (Deuteronomy 17:18).

In addition, make a mental note to write a reflection on this verse in a journal and meditate (recorded verbally, in writing, or by typing)

2. Calm Down:

Arrive at a place of stillness in God's presence, loving Him by worshiping Him with gentle music that soaks into my soul (2 Kings 3:15-16) and praying in tongues (1 Corinthians 14:15), while all the while smiling and imagining that Jesus is there in the upper room. (Acts 2:25). Tune yourself into the constant flow of ideas, images, and emotions from him (Jn. 7:37-39).

3. Reason:

Isaiah, 1:18 of the Bible says to "reason with God," which means that the Holy Spirit guides the train of our thoughts (i.e., through flow).

"Lord, what do You want to reveal to your people about the context of a passage, the Hebrew and Greek definitions of verse phrases, or cultural understandings?"

4. Speak and Imagine:

While reading the Bible aloud, you should try to visualize what you are reading in your mind by using the "eyes of your heart." Consider the biblical passage in question while quietly reciting it to yourselves until you can repeat it with your eyes shut. Take a mental note of the picture that appears in your mind's eye as you read the Scripture.

5. Feel the love of God:

As you pray over the image on the right, the Lord will ask you, "How does this Scripture communicate Your affection for us? " Try to get a sense of His heart and write down what you discover in your journal.

6. Hear the Rhema from God:

Put yourself in the situation described in this Bible passage and try to imagine what it would be in that situation. Your prayer should sound like this: "Lord, what are You trying to tell them with this Scripture?" Then, you should attune yourself to the flow of thoughts and flowing visuals (the voice and vision of God) and record that conversation in the two-way writing to keep for yourself.

7. Act:

Recognize the truth of the revelation, seek forgiveness for whatever offense you may have committed against it, and take vengeance on any opposition that stands in the way of its execution.

After that, it should be made public and then acted on immediately.

They asked each other, "Were not our hearts burning within us while he talked with us on the road and opened the Scriptures to us?" (Lk. 24:32).

And we all, who with unveiled faces contemplate the Lord's glory, are being transformed into his image with ever-increasing glory, which comes from the Lord, who is the Spirit. (2 Cor. 3:18).

Each solution will receive a relative weight based on the nature of the problem and God's will at this crossroads. The Holy Spirit is the one who is directing this work. Therefore, during all, continue to rely solely on Him.

REFERENCE

Acts 28:3 - KJV - And when Paul had gathered a bundle of sticks, and .... https://www.studylight.org/bible/eng/kjv/acts/28-3.html (Pg 34).

All Doubt – Quote Investigator https://quoteinvestigator.com/2010/05/17/remain-silent/ (Pg 86)

Anti-Christ Politics vs. the Politics of Jesus | Sojourners https://sojo.net/articles/anti-christ-politics-vs-politics-jesus (Pg 63).

Author DR. EBENEZER KYERE NKANSAH – Xulon Press. https://www.xulonpress.com/bookstore/bookdetail.php?PB_ISBN=9781545680636 (Pg 4)

Church of the Nations - Sun Stand Still: Prayer & Audacious Faith - COTN. https://www.cotn.org/gareth-hogg/474-sun-stand-still-prayer-a-audacious-faith (Pg 85).

God's Design for Man and Woman Book Review - CBMW. https://cbmw.org/2014/12/15/gods-design-for-man-and-woman-book-review/ (Pg. 75).

"'Have I Not Commanded You? Be Strong and of Good Courage; Do Not Be Afraid, nor Be Dismayed, for the Lord Your God Is with You Wherever You Go.'" Florida Times Union, Florida Times Union, 19 Sept. 2018, p. 1. (Pg 85).

How Do Cows Eat Their Food | Find Out Here | All Animals Faq. https://allanimalsfaq.com/cow/how-do-cows-eat-their-food/ (Pg 84).

Knock when turning steering wheel | Saabscene Saab Forum - Saab .... https://www.saabscene.com/threads/knock-when-turning-steering-wheel.131061 (Pg. 18).

Recognizing the Tactics of the Enemy | Bible.org. https://bible.org/seriespage/7-recognizing-tactics-enemy (Pg. 71, 74).

Rita Abena Amaniampong, (2022, 05/02), at 3:51 ET.

STRANGERS + EXILES: STANDING IN THE GAP. http://790fd854da554dce06bb-488e442c3101959db475c2d3bb12be0d.r37.cf2.rackcdn.com/uploaded/1/0e6339267_1498529311_170618-strangerexiles-standing-in-the-gap--keith.pdf (Pg 36).

What does Matthew chapter 26 mean? | BibleRef.com. https://www.bibleref.com/Matthew/26/Matthew-chapter-26.html (Pg 61).

What Each Zodiac Sign Is Unapologetically Picky About - YourTango. https://www.yourtango.com/2020331301/horoscope-most-picky-zodiac-signs-what-they-are-fussy-about-according-astrology (Pg 86).

What is the power of prayer? | GotQuestions.org. https://www.gotquestions.org/power-of-prayer.html Pg 9